The Grove

An East Texas Haunting

Mitchel Whitington

ISBN 978-1-9393062-5-8

First Edition

Printed in the United States of America
Published by 23 House Publishing
SAN 299-8084
www.23house.com

To Angie –

You talked your way into The Grove all those years ago, but stepped forever into our hearts and lives…

And to Stan –

Fellow Aggie, fellow brewmeister, fellow front porch philosopher; I'm always looking forward to our next evening at The Grove…

But most of all, to Audrey –

Each day you become more and more of a delightful young lady. I hope that as you continue to grow, your love for The Grove grows as well.

Table of Contents

The Grove, the first day that we saw it, 'For Sale' sign in front

Finding The Grove

I never set out to live in a "haunted" house – or whatever you'd call a place so active with the supernatural. No, that was not my intention. It just kind of worked out that way.

My wife and I both grew up in the town of Hooks, Texas, which is about an hour north of Jefferson. In fact, our cities were on-again, off-again high school football rivals. When it was time for a game, we'd come down Highway 59, drive through the 1960s neighborhood to get to the stadium, and then after the game, head back home. We never went into the historic district or knew a single thing about Jefferson's past.

A few years later we attended Texas A&M University at College Station, and the six-hour drive home took us through Jefferson, again on Highway 59. At its intersection with Highway 49 there was a traffic light, and on three of the four corners, there were gas stations – not a very picturesque memory of the city.

Years later we were living in the Dallas area and trying to find a place for a weekend getaway. A friend suggested Jefferson, and our first thought was, "The place with all the gas stations on the corner?" We kept hearing good things, though and even read a complimentary piece in the *Dallas Morning News*. With that, we made reservations at a historic, old hotel named "Excelsior House" and headed for East Texas.

We toured homes, took a boat ride down the bayou, ate at wonderful places, and spent a romantic evening seeing the city from a horse-drawn carriage. We fell in love with the little town immediately. One of the places that I'd found online was a restaurant set in an antebellum home called The Grove. It was reported to not only have delicious food, but a number of ghost stories as well. We went there for dinner one evening and found that it was closed – not just for that night, but for good. There even was a "for sale" sign out in front.

Even though we couldn't have the meal that we'd hoped for, we stood out in the street just staring at the house. As corny and contrived as this is going to sound, there was something about the place that was just calling to us. I hated that we couldn't eat there – I wanted to go inside, I wanted to explore every room, I wanted to know why the house suddenly seemed so important to me. There was an urgency to my emotion, and it was hard to get back in the car and drive away.

On the way out of town, we went back to the house for one more look and lingered a few moments before we headed home to the Dallas-Fort Worth Metroplex.

Jefferson was such a wonderful place that for the next year or so we came back several times to just get away from the hectic pace of everyday life, and in the course of our stay, we'd always find time to drive by The Grove.

On one trip, we called the number on the "for sale" sign and met the real estate agent. He unlocked the front door, and with more than a little excitement, we stepped across the threshold. I noticed immediately that it felt like home.

We took a lot of pictures that day so that we could go back and study the house, evaluate what areas might need work, and re-live the visit that we knew would be far too short.

The Front Parlor on the first day that we went inside

As we finally drove away, we took a reality check. We had a home in the Dallas suburb of Garland, we both had jobs in the Metroplex, and the most ridiculous idea in the world would be that we could buy The Grove in Jefferson.

But suddenly, strange things started happening to us. Not only did we begin having random thoughts and long conversations about the house, we started getting signs that pointed us to The Grove. Weird things... Tami got lost one day while taking a shortcut at lunch and looked up to see that she was on "Grove" street. She thought, "Awww, just a

3

coincidence." Then a week or so later she was stuck in traffic and there was a tractor-trailer in front of her hauling a piece of heavy equipment. The manufacturer of the huge tractor was a company named Grove, and it was plastered across the back of the machinery. There it was, "GROVE," in her line of sight from one side of her windshield to the other. We were both seeing the word "Grove" in the strangest places. Each time that one of us came home with another story, it would lead to another discussion about what color we might paint a room at The Grove, or what furniture we might want to use in the house, or some other aspect of ownership... even though we supposedly weren't even considering it.

Our local grocery store in Garland started a promotion where patrons could purchase a set of dishes over a period of several weeks. You could buy dinner plates one week, salad plates the next, and then soup bowls, etc. We thought that it would be a great set of everyday dishes, so we started picking them up as we bought groceries every week. As we were collecting the set, I happened to turn a plate over and see the brand – it was "Grove." Today they're still our everyday dishes.

We were heading back to our hometown of Hooks, Texas for a visit, and as we passed through the city of Mt. Pleasant on Interstate 30, I nodded toward one particular exit and said, "If we were going to Jefferson, that's the exit that we'd take!" That started another conversation about The Grove, of course. A minute later, Tami said that she'd like to stop and grab a soft drink and go to the bathroom, and since I'd just seen a sign for a McDonald's, I took the next exit.

As we were looking for the familiar Golden Arches, Tami noticed a street sign, and said, "You know how you were just talking about Jefferson? Well guess what street we're on right now – Jefferson Street!" We laughed at yet another strange occurrence, and the fact that we seemed to be getting a continuous string of signs and affirmations about The Grove.

4

At McDonald's I ordered the drinks while Tami excused herself to the ladies' room. When she came out, she had a funny look on her face.

"Everything all right?" I asked.

"The weirdest thing just happened…" as we stood there in line, she explained that she was in one of the bathroom stalls, and a woman came in with a little girl, and they were having a conversation that she really wasn't paying attention to. As they passed her, the little girl said, "Mom, there are signs everywhere…" Given all the affirmations that we'd been experiencing about The Grove, Tami wondered if this was just another one.

The strangest thing for me was that every time I was thinking about The Grove, I'd find a penny. This happened again and again, all in very odd places. It was strangely interesting, and I began to wonder why I was receiving signs like that. Years later, a psychic would tell me that my grandfather was sending me pennies as affirmations, and I suddenly remembered that as a child he'd always give me a penny to buy candy at the local grocery store – that was at a time when the concept of "penny candy" existed. Looking back, I have to believe that from his perch in the afterlife, Granddad was helping to steer me toward The Grove.

Things like this kept happening over and over throughout the year. I realize, of course, that the easiest thing in the world would be to say, "It was all coincidence; you guys were hyper-focused on The Grove, so of course you noticed any and everything that had that name attached to it."

During a phone conversation with my parents one evening, we were discussing Christmas plans, and out of nowhere my dad said, "I believe that we'll be decorating The Grove for Christmas this year!" I have no idea where that came from, but once we hung up the phone we spent an hour talking about how to deck the halls at The Grove.

5

As it turned out, we didn't get to do that… at least, not that year. But in November of 2001 I had a book signing in Tyler, so we decided to spend the weekend in Jefferson. We'd go check into the place we were staying, and then on Saturday afternoon we'd simply make the hour-long drive to Tyler. I'd do my gig, and then we would go back to have the rest of the weekend in our favorite city in the world.

That particular weekend we were staying at the historic old Jefferson Hotel, and we were in room 20 where we had quite a few paranormal experiences. Instead of frightening us away, we had a wonderful time.

My 2001 Book Signing in Tyler

We did the Tyler gig, and upon returning to Jefferson we had dinner at Lamache's Italian restaurant at the Jefferson Hotel. Afterwards we were both stuffed to the gills with delicious pasta and sauce, so we decided to take an evening

6

stroll… which of course, ended up with us walking toward The Grove. As we finally turned onto Moseley Street we could see the house a block away, and all of the lights were on, there were a couple of cars parked in front, and the "for sale" sign was gone. We both felt like we'd been kicked in the gut – we'd lost the house that we had been obsessing on for a couple of years.

I can't describe the overwhelming feeling of extreme disappointment that we had; it truly threw a damper on the entire weekend.

When we got back home, Tami called the real estate agent to ask when The Grove had sold. The agent said, "Oh, that house is not sellable; we can't find anyone who will buy it. I guess the owner is going to turn it into rental property."

That thought absolutely horrified us – The Grove deserved to have someone love it. Because of our schedules we couldn't just jump in the car and head back to Jefferson, but we did set up an appointment to see the house again on the first available weekend that we could.

To make a long story a little shorter, when that weekend arrived we traveled to Jefferson and went to the house one last time as visitors… because after that, on March 8, 2002, we became the latest owners of The Grove.

I've had a lifelong interest in the supernatural, so the stories of the ghosts there didn't bother me, and I didn't know if we'd even find them to be true. Tami and I simply embraced the house as our own. It had been sitting empty for a number of years, so the first weekend we set out to give it a good cleaning. It was a labor of love, as we started from the Front Parlor and worked our way back to the Kitchen. On that first night, we blew up an inflatable bed in the Front Parlor and turned in for the night… wondering what it might be like to sleep in a supposedly haunted house, of course.

We woke up the next morning refreshed from a good night of slumber. The sunlight was shining in through the thin, sheer curtains of the Front Parlor, and it looked like a beautiful spring day outside. We were sitting in bed talking and planning our day, and I asked Tami if she'd had any unusual experiences during the night. She laughed and said that she hadn't, but somewhere in the course of the evening she'd had an extremely vivid dream.

She said that in her dream she'd opened her eyes and saw two ladies standing outside in the darkness, looking through the sheer curtains at us. One was older, one was younger, and they both had beautiful, caramel skin. Between them was an illuminated figure eight, as if they were presenting it. Both were smiling and welcoming, and after a moment, they faded away. It would be several months before we discovered that we were the eighth owners of The Grove, and that the family who owned the house the longest were African-Americans. This gave substance to Tami's dream, and made us feel welcome.

The Front Parlor, where we slept the first night

Nothing else happened that first weekend that was in the least bit odd. It wasn't until a week later that I had my first experience. We brought two cars from Dallas that trip, each loaded down with everything from kitchen supplies to a window air conditioning unit. We'd become separated somewhere along the way, and I arrived at The Grove first, so I parked out on the street and started unloading my SUV.

At one point I carried a box in and put it on the table in the Game Room, when I heard something in the hall – footsteps, along with a strange noise. It sounded like someone had a couple of plastic bags from the grocery store and was walking down the hallway crinkling them together.

I assumed that Tami had arrived, and although I couldn't imagine why she'd come in the back door, it was obviously her walking down the hall carrying a bunch of sacks from her car. I stepped around the corner to give her a hand, and not only had the sounds stopped, but the hallway was empty. There was no mistaking what I'd heard, so I just stood there for a moment. About that time I heard the front door open and my wife called, "I'm here!"

Later I was relating the story to someone that we'd met in Jefferson, and she said, "What you could have been hearing were stiff petticoats rubbing together, like they used to wear in the olden days. We still wear them at festivals and such here in town, and if they're starched, that's exactly what they sound like."

The longer we owned The Grove, the more experiences we began to have. Footsteps in the Front Parlor, voices from somewhere nearby in the house, and shadows darting about that we'd usually see out of the corner of our eyes. Those, and many other things that we never thought to prepare ourselves for. All very different, all very strange.

But I'm writing this book to not only chronicle the history of the place, but to document the experiences that we've had –

and continue to have – at the beautiful, old house know as The Grove.

People are always asking me, "What's it like to live in a 'haunted house'?" In the pages of this book you'll find an answer to that question and more. Come with me on a journey into the supernatural. Put away your misconceptions and all the fabrications espoused by Hollywood.

The stories of The Grove that I want to share with you are not scary, evil, or frightening at all. In fact, I can think of only one word to describe them... true.

The Hallway where I first heard the footsteps and petticoats

*A typical grove of trees in the area – how
the property could have originally appeared*

Ancient History

Before there was a house called The Grove, before there was a Jefferson, before there was even a Texas, the first inhabitants of the region were the Caddo Indians, whose territory extended through East Texas, Louisiana, and Southern Arkansas. The name "Caddo" is derived from Kadohadacho, their actual name, and today refers to the confederacy of tribes of the area that shared a common language. Historians disagree on the exact number of tribes in the Caddo Confederacy, but they probably range between eight and twelve groups, and encompassed several thousand people.

Unlike other native cultures, the Caddo weren't nomadic. They established villages and were very adept at farming, hunting, and fishing. Deer was a primary meat source, although

11

the Caddo also hunted bear, birds, and small animals such as rabbits, mice, and snakes.

To travel for hunting and such, the Caddo used rivers and streams like we use highways and roads. They would have definitely made use of the Big Cypress Bayou, the river that runs on the south boundary of Jefferson, and the one that is only about two hundred yards from The Grove.

When it came to burying their dead, the Caddo were not that different than people today. According to Jefferson historian Mildred S. Gleason in her book *Caddo: A Survey of Caddo Indians in Northeast Texas and Marion County*, the body of a departed Caddo tribe member was washed and then displayed in state in his or her dwelling while the family grieved.

At the burial, the body was laid to rest facing east toward the rising sun. The deceased was buried with food, weapons, pottery, trophies and anything else that might prove useful in the afterlife.

The Caddo believed that the spirit stayed in the body for six days and nights, so a fire of cedar and mulberry was kept burning for that period. A feast was held to honor the dead one, and a full serving of the meal was placed on the center of the grave to nourish the deceased on their journey

Like modern man does today, the Caddo would often designate certain sites as burial areas, and often grouped graves together. This has been proven by excavations that have taken place around East Texas, including along the Big Cypress River.

In her book, Ms. Gleason goes on to describe that the Caddo inhabited the area that is now Jefferson, Texas. Published maps of the Big Cypress Bayou area show that there are a plethora of Caddo burial sites around the area that is now Jefferson. Given this evidence, it isn't hard to imagine at all that a grove of Native Texas Pecan trees would be a preferred location – after all, the deceased would have a continual supply of food in the afterlife, in the form of the pecans.

But why would someone even contemplate that? Well, read on...

The Bodies on the Property

As soon as we bought The Grove, we began hearing stories about it from the people in Jefferson right away. It seemed like everyone we met had a ghostly tale of one form or another to relate. One thing that we kept hearing over and over was that there were bodies buried on the property. As it turned out, we didn't just hear this from the folks in town, but from strangers who visited there as well.

For example, one Sunday morning I was sweeping off the front porch, getting ready for a tour later in an hour or so, when a car stopped in front of the house and a man got out. This was before the property was fenced, so he simply walked up into the garden and started looking around.

I propped my broom against a chair and went down the front steps. As I did, I spoke to the fellow. "Hi – how's it going?"

He hadn't noticed me, so he was a little startled but finally said, "I'm sorry, I didn't mean to intrude. I just wanted to get a look at The Grove that I've heard so much about."

I told him about the upcoming tour, but he said that he was regrettably heading out of town and wouldn't be able to stay for it.

He was a nice guy, though, so we stood and talked about the house for quite a while. Finally, he glanced down at his watch and said, "Well, I've got to go, but before I do I have a question." After a pause, he continued. "Where are the bodies buried?"

His question caught me off guard and I probably looked surprised, but finally managed to say, "What?"

He smiled and said, "I should have told you earlier, but I'm a psychic. I'm getting a lot of good feelings from your house, but I am definitely picking up on the fact that there are bodies buried on the property."

I told him that although we'd heard rumors and such, as far as I knew, there weren't really any bodies interred at The Grove.

He had a knowing expression on his face as he looked around the garden. Finally, he said, "Thanks for letting me stop by, but I guess I've got to get on the road."

We talked a little more as he headed back to his car. Before he got inside, he looked back and said, "But there really are bodies buried here."

I couldn't help but think about that as I went back to my sweeping.

A year or so went by, and a lady called for a tour of the house. It was during the off-season in Jefferson, so she and her friend were the only ones that day. Before we went inside the house, she announced to me that she was a psychic. I asked her to please tell me about anything that she picked up on and welcomed her into the house

We spent the next hour going through all the rooms, and she had many fascinating comments – some that I could confirm, and others that were new to me.

After we finished the tour and were standing on the front porch, she added, "By the way, you do know that you have bodies buried here, right?"

I told her that while that subject had come up before, I really had no confirmation of it.

She was quiet for a moment, thinking about it, and then said, "What I'm picking up on is that these burials didn't have anything to do with The Grove. They happened long before the house was ever built."

I thought that was very interesting, but when she left I just filed that away in my mind for future reference.

14

A third psychic that visited the house came with a paranormal investigation group that we had invited to The Grove, and she was very good. She accurately pinpointed many areas of activity with no prior knowledge of the house, and told us a number of things that we were later able to verify. A lot of people claim to have psychic powers, but this woman was the real deal.

As she was going over her findings with us while sitting in the Front Parlor of The Grove, she said, "…and there are bodies buried on the property."

I didn't say anything, but let her continue.

The psychic went on to say, "They're not connected to the house; from what I'm picking up on, I believe that they are Native American." She went on to say that she was picking up on a few of them standing at the back of the property, watching as she walked around – as if they knew that she could sense them.

That was the third time I'd been told about graves at The Grove, by three completely different people, at three completely different times. I hadn't shared the "bodies on the property" story with anyone but my wife, so other than some rumors around town, nobody had any reason to talk about the bodies – certainly nothing as specific as Native American burials.

There are no marked graves on the property, but a few things about the words of the three psychics intrigued me.

But all this is circumstantial evidence – nothing concrete at all. When I was discussing this with Patrick Hopkins, the former owner of The Grove, however, he had some additional information that was very interesting.

A number of years ago one of the largest pecan trees on the property had fallen over during an ice storm, and when he was looking at the crater left by the massive root ball, Patrick found a piece of Native American pottery several feet down. Because it was so deep in the ground he couldn't help but wonder whether it was part of a grave… and if The Grove was built on a Caddo burial ground. I pondered that for a moment and mentally added the information to the things that the psychics said.

A couple of years after that we had a deluge of rain that seemed to go on for a week, and when it was finally over I was working out in the yard and saw something that caught my eye – a piece of pottery partially visible in the soil. I could see that it had a pattern of lines etched into it.

A pottery fragment found at The Grove

It had obviously been buried, but enough of the soil had been washed away from it for me to spot it. I took it inside the house, did some research online, and found that it was very similar to Caddo Indian pieces.

Fast-forward another year or so and my wife and I were working out in the garden, putting out some new plants, and I was digging a hole that was at least a foot down, maybe a little more. I hit something solid, and when I dug it out, it was a large, L-shaped piece of pottery shown below. The bottom was blackened as if it had been used to cook over many fires.

It interested me so much that I continued to dig around the area, but couldn't find any more pieces of the pottery. I would love to have found enough to reconstruct it, but that didn't happen.

The rough exterior of another piece pottery on the left,
and the smooth interior on the right.

It happened again a year or so later. Again, I was digging a hole, and found a piece of pottery that was irregularly thick on the bottom, but the outside was smooth and polished as if it had been fired.

Stepping back and looking at the whole "burial ground" thing, I know that a skeptic would first of all throw out everything from the psychics, and then say, "Three pieces of pottery does not a burial ground make."

Still, it's hard for me to ignore that three different people with psychic abilities, a year or more apart, without knowing each other or what any of the others said, all felt that there were graves on the property.

And in the meantime, again, years apart and under very different circumstances, Indian pottery was found in the ground at The Grove. As much as I know that people would like to discount all that, I at least have to give it a nod of credibility.

The third piece of pottery that was found buried at The Grove

But what if The Grove was once a burial ground? Does that explain the supernatural happenings there? Not necessarily… but I do believe that cemeteries are sacred places, and that might be a reason that the property seems to be a conduit for the paranormal.

There is definitely a stigma attached to such a concept. The problem is that when Hollywood gets hold of an idea like a home being built on a burial ground, it takes the premise and runs amok. Take the horror classic *Poltergeist* from 1982, with Steven Spielberg as one of the writers and producers, and a driving force behind the film. As a terror film it's a definitive part of the genre, and since it grossed $132 million at the U.S. box office, you can see that it was a popular movie.

The plot is that a housing addition was built on top of a cemetery, and the spirits of the people who were buried there wreak havoc on an innocent family. With great special effects and lots of chills, it's a must-see for the ghost-movie buff.

In addition to *Poltergeist*, a number of other movies have the exact same plot device... a house built on a burial ground. Here are some of the titles: *Pet Sematary*, *Amityville Horror*, *Identity*, *The Shining*, *Buffy the Vampire Slayer*, *Scalps*, and *The Legacy of Hilltop Drive* to name but a few.

In almost every case, the haunting in the movie is caused by the spirits of the burial ground coming up to punish the living for building on their graves.

But in reality, I have *never* seen a real-world situation where something that sinister happened... and it certainly hasn't at The Grove. If there are Caddo Indian graves here, I would assume that it has only made the place more spiritual, and perhaps provided a conduit for a link to the other side.

Any such burials on the property would make The Grove hallowed ground, and I can live with that. If that spirituality presents a portal for supernatural activity, I'm okay with that as well. We've never been frightened, never felt anything evil, and in fact, have found The Grove to be a place full of love, acceptance, and occasionally a little mischief.

Whatever the Caddo Indians were using the area for all those centuries, however, would soon be buried, as the wheels of progress began to turn.

Settlers made their way up Big Cypress Bayou from Louisiana, a man named Allen Urquhart established a ferry across the river, and soon a post office was established in the area.

Urquhart and another land investor named Daniel Alley purchased two halves of the property that would eventually become the City of Jefferson. The steamboats found their way up Big Cypress Bayou, and more and more people came to the area to establish a home.

19

Steamboats in port (Courtesy the Library of Congress)

Before The Grove

The house was built in 1861, but there were three owners of the property prior to that... which may explain why at least one aspect of our supernatural activity takes place outside of the house.

In today's world, there is a ghostly man in a dark suit that is seen wandering the area that is now the garden, but was once a yard to the first house. He is rarely seen inside The Grove, however.

It may be that he is associated with the property before the current house was built, which warrants a discussion of what was on the land prior to The Grove.

The Alley Years, 1842-1847

When Daniel and Lucy Alley purchased 586 acres of land from the Stephen Smith Land Grant in 1842, it included the property that would become The Grove.

Daniel Alley

21

While the Alleys owned The Grove property – along with pretty much everything surrounding it – Captain William Perry brought the very first stern-wheeler up the Great Cypress Bayou into the settlement that would eventually become Jefferson, signaling the start of the city's history as a river port. In 1844 when he came into town, Captain Perry saw the potential in the port city. He had a vision of a thriving place, and built the Excelsior House as a hotel for the genteel travelers on the river.

Excelsior House – photo circa 1930

Two years prior to Captain Perry's arrival, on August 9, 1842, Mr. Charles Ames was married to Mrs. Harriet Potter by Rev. Samuel Corley. This is significant because Amos Morrill, the next owner of The Grove property, would become Ms. Potter's attorney in her famous legal battles against her former husband's estate. Speaking of the Honorable Judge Morrill, it's time to take a look at his life in Jefferson.

The Morrill Years, 1847-1855

Amos Morrill purchased The Grove property from Daniel and Lucy Alley in 1847, and he was reportedly a very interesting character.

The Federal Judicial Center Homepage contains the following information about Morrill: He was born on August 25, 1809, in Salisbury, MA, and died on March 5, 1884, in Austin, TX. Morrill was educated at Bowdoin College in Maine, graduating in 1834, and then moved to Tennessee and taught at Murfreesboro for two years. He opened a private practice in Murfreesboro that he kept until 1839, at which time he moved to Texas to practice law there.

Judge Amos Morrill

The First House on the Property

From 1839 until 1856, Morrill maintained a private practice in Clarksville, Texas. During that time, he purchased The Grove property and the entire block on which it is located from Daniel Alley in 1847, building a dog run style log cabin on the southwest corner of the property.

Typical "Dog Run" Cabin Architecture (author's collection)

Although his office in Clarksville was ninety miles away, he maintained his Jefferson house so that he could practice law there as well.

Harriet Potter Ames recorded in her autobiography that she enlisted the service of Morrill, along with her husband Charles Ames, in her court case to claim her fair share of her late husband's estate that he'd left to a mistress. There were literally years of pleadings in the case, which was tried in Marion County District Court, and judgment was eventually rendered in Harriet's favor. The case was appealed by the estate of Sophia Mayfield, however, and was reversed and remanded by the Texas Supreme Court in 1875. Although they lost the case, it ultimately laid the groundwork for future cases that would ensure the property rights of women in marriage.

Amos Morrill was never a lawyer who shied away from controversy. But while he had the reputation of a ruthless counselor, he fought hard for his clients. In 1861, Morrill was approached by Priscilla Harrison, a slave who had been freed in her master's will. Amos Morrill greatly opposed slavery, but upon hearing the woman's story, decided to take the case. She had found that the life of a free, unmarried black woman was almost too much to bear. There were no jobs available because slavery was still active in the country – people were unwilling to pay money to a woman for a job that a slave could be made to do for free. In order to provide food and shelter for her children, Priscilla took the only course of action that was available to her: return to a life of slavery. When she enlisted the help of Amos Morrill, he was able to use a newly enacted Texas law that allowed freed slaves to become a slave once again, but to name their masters. She chose a kind family named Johnston, and when the Emancipation Proclamation freed her once again, she chose to stay and work for the Johnstons until all of the original family members had passed away.

Morrill was absent from Texas during the Civil War years. Because of his opposition to slavery and to secession, when the war broke out he left the state and rode out the turbulent years in the north. Upon returning to Texas to resume his practice of law, Morrill was appointed Chief justice of the Texas Supreme Court in 1868, a position that he held for two years.

His Federal Judicial Service consists of the U. S. District Court, Eastern District of Texas, to which he was nominated by Ulysses Grant on January 18, 1872, to a seat vacated by Joel C. C. Winch. His seat was confirmed by the Senate on February 5, 1872, and he received the commission on February 5, 1872. Morrill's Service terminated on October 18, 1883, when he retired.

The Encyclopedia of the New West of Texas, Arkansas, Colorado, New Mexico and Indian Territory, published in

1881, ended its listing of Judge Amos Morrill with the following words: "He is now about seventy-two years of age, in fine health, and in fine mental vigor. In person, he is a man of good presence and large frame, always a welcome guest in the social circle – a good conversationalist and a man of able thought."

Amos Morrill would die three years later in Austin, Texas, having lived a full life of both prosperity and service.

While Amos Morrill owned The Grove property, a wonderful thing happened in East Texas: on March 20, 1848, the town of Jefferson was incorporated. The next owner would play a large part in the real estate of the new town.

The Ragin Years, 1855-1861

On March 17, 1855, Caleb Ragin and his wife, Sarah Wilson Ragin, bought The Grove property from Amos Morrill.

At that time, Caleb had already established himself as a prominent citizen of Jefferson. According to the Cass County Genealogical Society's history of Jefferson in their publication *The Jefferson, Texas Cemeteries*, Caleb served as the official postmaster for the city from December 31, 1849, to August 4, 1851.

On the 1850 census, Caleb was listed as a white male, a grocery merchant who was born in South Carolina. His wife Sarah was recorded as being a white female who was born in Arkansas.

Caleb and Sarah were married on December 11, 1849, according to Cass County marriage records. Miss Sara Wilson was the daughter of Colonel John Wilson, and officiating at the ceremony was Rev. B.B. Dyes.

An interesting story about Sarah Wilson Ragin is not about her, but instead, regarding her father. Back in Arkansas, Colonel John Wilson was the Judge Advocate of the Militia, President of the first Arkansas Constitutional Convention, President of the Real Estate Bank (the first bank in Arkansas), and speaker of the House of Representatives of the first General Assembly of the State of Arkansas. The following account of Col. Wilson comes from the archives of the Old State House in Arkansas, and the 12/16/1937 edition of *The Charlotte News*, which published the account of the event that happened one hundred years before.

Back in 1837, during the very first legislative assembly, a bill was introduced on the floor to offer bounty fees for the pelts of timber wolves. Major J.J. Anthony, the Randolph County representative, seemed to be opposed to the bill because he mused that if such a law was enacted, the pelts would become tradable commodities much like currency. He went on to add a sarcastic remark that perhaps a local magistrate shouldn't pay the bounty for the wolves, but instead, the President of the Real Estate Bank should handle the task personally, signing the pelts to make them legal tender. Colonel Wilson took offense to this and asked from the podium whether or not Major Anthony meant the remark as an insult. Anthony replied, "I believe there should be more dignity attached to the office of one who receives oaths in the state of Arkansas."

Colonel Wilson was incensed at the remark and leaped from the podium to challenge Major Anthony physically. Wilson drew his nine-inch Bowie knife, and Anthony pulled out his own, a twelve-incher. A fight ensued, and after Major Anthony slashed Col. Wilson on the forearm, Wilson buried his knife in Anthony's chest – the man died on the floor of the House of Representatives.

Wilson was tried and cleared on the account of "excusable homicide," after which he invited the entire courtroom to drink with him at a local bar. He won the day, but had been stripped of his seat in the house and in fact had lost most of his political power. He moved his family to Texas for a new beginning, and appears on the census of Harrison County with his daughter Sarah, before her marriage to Caleb Ragin.

Arkansas House of Representatives Chamber (author's photo)

Caleb and Sarah lived on the property that would eventually become The Grove for six years. Although they sold it to the Stilleys in 1861, the couple and their family apparently stayed in Jefferson. The following entry appears in the 1880 Census:

```
1880 Census, Marion County
Family 98
Caleb Ragin (Male-60), White, Farmer, Born SC
Sarah Ragin (Female-53), White, Born AR
Burlee Ragin (Male-26), White, Farmer, Born TX
Mrs. Eva Ragin (Female-21), White, Born AL
Clement Ragin (Male-8 mo.), White, Born TX
```

At the time of that census, Arzella Ragin, Caleb and Sarah's daughter, had already passed away (as reflected in the cemetery records below). Burlee, their son, would also die that year on August 10, after the census had been taken. Their family plot can be found in Oakwood Cemetery, with the following four markers:

```
Caleb Ragin - b. 10/14/1820, d. 9/12/1884
Sarah Ragin - b. 2/24/1828, d. 9/2/1898
Burlee Ragin - b. 8/10/1854, d. 8/10/1880
Arzella Ragin - b. 10/15/1850, d. 11/27/1869
```

Ragin Family Markers in Oakwood Cemetery

The Ragins both outlived their children, and when Caleb died, Sarah carved the epitaph on his tombstone:

In Memory of My Husband – We will meet again.

Instead of staying in Jefferson and managing the family business, Sarah decided to move to Mansfield, Texas in 1887. She died in 1898 in Mansfield, and her body was returned to

29

Oakwood Cemetery to be buried with the rest of her family. To complete the inscription that had been placed on her husband's tombstone, Sarah had requested that hers be inscribed with the epitaph:

We Met Again

The Garden Guy

Before we move on to the house itself, there is one spirit that I should mention. We see him in the garden occasionally, and he is very interactive – looking at you, smiling, and so forth. Interestingly enough he rarely comes inside the house.

I have to wonder if that is because in his world, the house doesn't exist. He could have lived on the property at a time before the house was built, which could mean that he is Amos Morrill or Caleb Ragin. There's no way to be sure, but since it is a likely possibility, I thought that this would be the place to introduce him.

We were leaving one afternoon to go grab a bite to eat, and we walked out of the side door at the back of the house.

As we exited the side door, I glanced over toward the back of the property, and there was a well-dressed man in the backyard. He was wearing a black suit and old-fashioned hat, and had a mischievous grin on his face as if to say, "Look at me! I'm in your backyard! Now, what are you gonna do about it?"

That instantly alarmed and angered me, so I ducked back into the house, dashed the short distance to the back door, and threw it open. I was ready to confront that cocky fellow... but he wasn't standing in the backyard, jumping over the fence, or running away. There was simply no one there.

I shut the back door and joined my wife. As I closed the side door behind me, she said, "What was all that about?"

I explained about the guy in the backyard who suddenly wasn't there.

"Are you sure that you saw him?" she asked.

"Positive."

She laughed, and said, "Then you better call Patrick."

Patrick Hopkins was the chef who had a restaurant at the house in the 1990s. I called him on the phone when we got back, and started out by saying, "Hi Patrick, it's Mitchel, and I just saw the strangest thing out in the garden of The Grove..."

"Let me guess," he said without missing a beat. "It was a man dressed in a black suit, and he was laughing or smiling at you."

His quick answer took me aback, but after a moment I said, "Yeah, that's exactly what I saw."

With a chuckle, he said, "That's the Garden Guy – he turns up from time to time. Not only does he look like a real person, until he just vanishes, that is, but he's always got a smile on his face. He seems to be quite the jovial fellow."

We spoke a little bit longer before I hung up and related our conversation to my wife. I think that both of us wondered what kind of adventures might be in store for us as the new owners.

Over the years, he's been spotted many times. I've seen him in different parts of the garden just walking along at a good clip. Either he'll pass behind a tree and not come out from the other side, or simply fade away. Sometimes he's looking at me, other times he is staring straight ahead as he goes.

A few times our friends have seen him as well. On one occasion, a buddy of mine told us, "I came by yesterday and was going to stop, but I saw that you had company."

No one but us had been there the day before, so that confused me. "What do you mean?" I asked.

"I was about to pull over and park in front of the house when I noticed a guy walking around the garden. I didn't recognize him, so I figured that you had someone visiting, so I just kept going."

I couldn't help but smile as I explained that we were inside the house having a quiet afternoon alone.

The Front of the Grove Gardens, Where He Often Walks

We don't usually talk about the Garden Guy on the tour anymore because there are so many other stories to tell – if we included all of our stories, the tour might be six hours long. Anyway, after one of the tours, a gentleman asked me who the man in the garden was. Since I hadn't mentioned him, I wondered if he'd read about him in a book or something like that. As it turned out, though, the fellow said that he'd seen the Garden Guy during the restaurant days of The Grove. They were standing out in the garden and looked up to see a man out there simply standing among the plants and smiling. The visitor and his companion turned to look at each other, and then glanced back to see that the man had disappeared.

That's our Garden Guy, though. We have no idea who it could be – Morrill, Ragin, or whoever else... perhaps one of these days we'll get a clue as to who he is, but for now, we'll just enjoy his occasional appearances!

*The Grove on the 1872 Brosius Map of Jefferson
(courtesy Jefferson Historical Society and Museum)*

Building The Grove:
The Stilley Years 1861-1880

Since we've owned The Grove, on a couple of different occasions we've had a call from someone who said, "I'm a relative of the man who built your house – Washington Frank Stilley." Of course, we're always anxious to learn more about the history of the house, so we not only welcomed them on the tour but invited them to stay for a visit afterward.

We've been able to piece together a history of the house from the Stilley family, from research that the seventh owner, Patrick Hopkins, has given us, and from doing a lot of digging on our own.

To understand the history of The Grove, you first have to look at the history of the City of Jefferson. In the mid-1800s, it was the second-largest waterport entry into Texas. Where there are now quaint little stores and antique shops, in the 1800s some of those same buildings housed saloons, dance halls, and brothels. There were parts of town that were more than a little rough.

A young man named Washington Frank Stilley had an office and storefront downtown, and he was both a merchant and a cotton factor (which we might call a cotton broker today). Not only did he sell general merchandise, but he would purchase cotton from the growers and plantation owners in the area, have it ginned and baled, and then ship it to the mills in the east to be turned into textiles. As a young man, Frank did quite well for himself.

A newspaper ad for Frank Stilley

As the story goes, one day Frank ran across a young lady downtown, and three things about her caught his attention. The first was that she was a very attractive young lady; the second was that he saw she was not wearing a wedding ring on her finger, and the third was that she was being escorted around town not by a young man, but instead by an older gentleman that he took to be her father.

Frank reasoned that if she was strolling about town without a young man on her arm, she might be available. He began to make inquiries about her and learned that her name was Minerva Fox, from the Fox Plantation in Marshall, Texas.

Days went by, and Frank couldn't get Minerva off his mind. He finally got on his horse and made the long horseback ride to the Fox Plantation in Marshall – fifteen whole miles – where he went to call on Mr. Fox.

In those days a young man had to first obtain permission from the father of the family before courting a young lady. A lot of dads that I run across today don't think that this is an altogether bad idea.

Frank sat down to visit with Mr. Fox, introduced himself and expressed his interest in courting Minerva. Mr. Fox was more or less interviewing this young man to see if he might be a good candidate for his daughter. When he learned what Frank did for a living, the wheels in Mr. Fox's head started turning.

The largest crop on the Fox Plantation was cotton, and so Mr. Fox realized that if Frank and Minerva got together, he would get a son-in-law whose specialty was selling that crop.

Mr. Fox not only gave his permission but encouraged the relationship. The young couple started dating, fell in love, and were married on June 21, 1860, in Jefferson, officiated by Rev. Sol O'Dell as noted in the Marion County marriage records. Mr. Fox purchased the property on November 13, 1861, for the couple, and construction was started on a house for the newlyweds, a wedding gift from Mr. Fox, and it was completed in 1861 with all the trappings of a fine residence of the day. The young couple moved into The Grove to begin their married life together.

Although his father-in-law paid for the house – and put it in his wife's name – Frank left his mark on The Grove. The exterior architecture is Greek Revival, a very symmetrical style as witnessed by the front porch and the columns. It was very popular across the South, as well as East Texas. If the interior of the house was also Greek Revival, however, there would be a long hallway down the center of the house with matching rooms on either side.

The Grove wasn't built like that because the interior of the house is in Creole Architecture.

Creole is one of only a few architectural styles that originated right here in the United States. There are a number of Creole attributes to the interior of the house, not the least of which is the fact that there is no main hallway – they thought that hallways were a waste of space. In a Creole home like The Grove, someone must walk from room to room to go through the house. It also included front and side galleries that were under the main roof of the house, no main connecting hallway, and a basic ell-shaped floor plan.

This combination of Greek Revival that was popular in East Texas, and Creole from Louisiana, makes The Grove a perfect reflection of the combination of cultures in Jefferson during the mid-1800s. This architectural marriage was one of the reasons that the Department of the Interior placed the house on the National Register of Historic Places.

When we first purchased The Grove, we had a bit of work to do on it. Chef Patrick Hopkins had done a restoration of the house that saved it, but since it had been sitting empty for a number of years, we had to give it some tender loving care as well.

In the process, we basically turned the front porch into a workshop, with a table saw at one end, all of our tools laid out, and lumber stacked up on the other. As we worked on the house, people from town who were out walking would stop and introduce themselves. They'd always ask us the same question: "Are you guys turning The Grove into a bed and breakfast?"

We'd laugh and say, "No, 'cause if we did, you'd have to walk through everyone else's room to get to yours, so you'd have to know your neighbors really, really well!"

Even though it wouldn't make a very good B&B, the Stilleys built a wonderful place to live.

Frank's business was mentioned in the Harrison Flag newspaper in Marshall, Texas in 1865:

The Harrison Flag, Marshall, Texas 11/22/65

W.F. Stilley and Co., Jefferson, Texas. – We take pleasure in directing public attention to the advertisement of this firm. They keep on hand a large assortment of goods, and of the best quality. We have known Mr. Frank Stilley in business, and have proven him to be a clever accommodating gentleman. We bespeak for this firm a liberal share of public patronage.

Frank and Minerva had two sons while living at The Grove: John R. (born 1869) and Frank, Jr. (born 1870). Apparently, the Stilleys needed more space for their new family, because in 1870 they expanded the Master Bedroom, added a room onto the back of the house to join it to the Kitchen, and also an open side porch running the length of the house that looked out into the garden. The new configuration of the house is shown on a map of Jefferson that was hand-drawn by a mapmaker named H. Brosius and hangs in the Jefferson Historical Museum. The Grove, on the Brosius map, was shown at the first of this chapter.

Things may not have been completely smooth for Frank Stilley through the years. In the 1860s, he is reported to have established a cotton warehouse in Jefferson, which was destroyed in a flood of the Big Cypress Bayou in 1866. While this has not been verified, something apparently did happen to his business because the 1870 census lists him as a clerk. Or perhaps the "clerk" designation applies to someone who owns their own business.

The exact census record states:

```
1870 Census of Marion County
Family 329
Frank W. Stilley (Male-35), White, Clerk, Born LA
Minerva Stilley (Female-33), White, Keeping House,
    Born NC
John R. Stilley (Male-1), White, Born TX
Frank Stilley (Male-6 mo), White, Born TX
```

The Stockade Case and The Grove

On October 4, 1868, a terrible event happened in Jefferson that apparently involved The Grove. A Yankee carpetbagger named George Webster Smith who was living in Jefferson had a political meeting involving the freedmen of the city. It apparently angered much of the town's citizenry, because the local sheriff advised Smith and four of the leading freedmen to spend the night in the city's jail for their own protection.

That night, masked riders from a local organization known as the Knights of the Rising Sun came to the jail – known as the calaboose – and demanded that Smith and the four freedmen be released to them.

Overpowering the deputies, the Knights shot and killed Smith in the calaboose, and took the four freedmen away to be hanged. Since the calaboose was at the corner of Line and Lafayette streets, they took the men one street down to Moseley and led them away from town toward a place known as Sulfur Springs where the executions would take place. As they dragged them down Moseley Street, all of the freedmen struggled to free themselves. Two escaped, and the mob abandoned the idea of hanging the others and decided to kill them on the spot instead – presumably there on Moseley Street.

One account of the evening states that as they were struggling with the other two freedmen, a man came out of a house and said, "There is a sick woman here – can you please take this somewhere else?"

The other two freedmen were finally shot, and in the following days, arrests were made, which included most of the men of the town who were in the Knights of the Rising Sun. A wooden stockade was built to house all the accused.

When the Union troops occupying Jefferson held a trial, a map was drawn of all of the significant locations, and the only place on Moseley Street that was noted on the map was The Grove, which was listed as "Mr. Stilley's House."

It is therefore not a far stretch at all to extrapolate that the house where the freedmen were being killed was The Grove, and the man asking the mob to move on was Mr. Stilley. While we can't be sure, it's the only explanation that makes sense, which could mean that the two men were murdered in front of the house, or even on the property as they ran away.

The End of the Stilley Era

Unfortunately, the love story of the Stilleys came to an end. Marriage records indicate that Frank Stilley married Sarah Butler on February 3, 1876, and at some point moved to Weatherford, Texas. In 1879, Minerva Fox Stilley died. Since the property was in her sons' names, it was sold by a trusteeship for them. We can't find any further records of Frank or Minerva, or their children, which is an unfortunate fact for these pages of The Grove's history. From the information that we have, it appears that Frank and Minerva divorced, and Frank remarried. Since the house was in Minerva's name when she died, it passed to her heirs, John and Frank, Jr.

In the book *Cemetery Records of Marion County, Texas* by Martha McGraw Chapter D.A.R., Jefferson, Texas, 1961, on page 252, the following entry is found in the Burial Records of Oakwood Cemetery:

Vol/Page Name Age Burial Block
4-50 John R. STILLEY (at Greenville) 23 Dec. 16,
1891

From this entry, it seems likely that John died in Greenville, and his body was returned to be buried with his mother in Oakwood Cemetery.

The Stilley family will be remembered as the people who built the house as it stands today. In the archives of the Jefferson Historical Society and Museum, the February 1960 book entitled, *A Partial List of Earlier Citizens of Jefferson, Texas, Compiled From Memory* by Gustav Frank II mentions The Grove property: "Stilley Family – Res Block D, Lot 9, Moseley Street. Mr. Stilley was a contractor. Many years later this house was occupied by Charlie Young, a colored barber." Mr. Frank closes the book with the notation that the information comes from his memory, in some cases from over sixty years prior, which may explain his indication of Frank Stilley as a contractor. He has been recorded as a cotton broker, and then a merchant in the census records, but was never recorded as a contractor in any other historical records. The "colored barber" from Frank's memory is none other than Mr. Charlie Young, a leader in the African-American community in Jefferson during his day. He is discussed in a later chapter in this book.

The Lady in White

And as long as we're covering the Stilleys, it's probably time to talk about the famous "Lady in White" at The Grove.

We first learned about her when we were looking at the house on the second occasion when the current owner Chef Patrick Hopkins was there. He told us a fascinating story...

During the restaurant days, Patrick was doing a number of things to promote the business. One of them was dinner theater, where a group of actors performed a play while the meal was being served. The play was an old-fashioned murder mystery called *Angel Street*, and so everyone was dressed in period costume.

During a full-dress rehearsal one evening, the lighting tech had her control board set up out on the front porch so that it wouldn't take up space in the Dining Room. She was working the lights as the rehearsal progressed when she glanced over to the east side of the house and saw a lady in a long, white dress walking toward the back.

The lighting tech called out, "Excuse me – you're going the wrong way!"

The woman seemed not to notice and kept walking.

The lighting tech yelled again, "Hey, lady, I'm trying to tell you! There's no door on that side of the house. You're going the wrong way!"

Again, the woman just kept walking as if nothing had been said and disappeared behind the back corner of the porch.

This intrigued the lighting tech to the point that she walked over to the railing, leaned over, and tried to get this woman's attention one more time.

"Hey lady," she yelled, "I'm trying to tell you that..."

At that point, the lady in the white dress took a left and stepped up through a wall of the house.

Meanwhile, back inside of the house, the actors and actresses were going through the paces of the play. One actress was on the landing of the staircase, getting ready to make her grand entrance when she looked into what is now the Game Room and saw a lady in a long white dress walking towards her.

She thought she knew all the actresses, yet here was a stranger. As the woman walked across the Stairwell in front of her, the actress said, "Excuse me, are you supposed to be here? The restaurant is closed for the evening..."

The woman just ignored her and walked into the far room.

The actress thought, "How rude!" and went down the stairs and into the room after her to see who this was. When she got inside, she found the room to be completely empty. There was no other way in or out of the room, so she realized what she must have seen. She ran back up front where the other actors were, and said, "You're not going to believe what I just saw! You're not going to believe what I just saw!"

About that time, the lighting tech from the front porch came bursting through the front door, saying, "You're not going to believe what I just saw!"

The ladies saw two halves of the same event: a woman in a long white dress was walking along the east side of The Grove, and then took a left to step up through a wall of the house. Inside, she crossed the interior to go into what was once the Children's Bedroom.

As I said, Patrick told us the story, and when I first heard it, what he said really didn't make any sense to me – why would this spirit be stepping up through a wall?

In my writing career I've visited haunted places all around the country: investigating, interviewing, and researching. Over all these years, one of the things that I've come to believe is that there is a continuity between our world and the next. These spirits might be checking on people, places, or things that were important to them in life... things that were familiar to them. I've never found it to be like in the cartoons, where ghosts pop back and forth through walls for no reason at all.

I just dismissed the story and went on looking at the house that day. We bought The Grove, of course, and it wasn't long until we began having our own experiences with the Lady in White.

But then I started to study the architecture of The Grove – and a lot of this information was provided by Patrick. During the restaurant days he'd done a tremendous amount of research on the house and collected a lot of oral history from the people of Jefferson.

He pointed out to me that in the Game Room, there is a beam that crosses towards the back on the ceiling, and that it is where the back of the house used to be. Originally it had only five rooms: A parlor and dining room up front, and two bedrooms with a family utility area between them in back.

The Stilleys expanded the room in 1870, adding five or six feet onto what was their bedroom at the time. It is now our game room, and the place where the Lady in White steps up through the wall.

The Game Room, showing the beam running across the ceiling and down the wall. The print and shelf is where the Lady in White enters the room.

Prior to the Stilley addition, there was a back porch on that side of the house. When I realized that, the Lady in White's path made perfect sense. She's probably not stepping up through a wall of the house, but instead stepping up onto a back porch that was there prior to 1870.

If that is the case, the famous "Lady in White" of The Grove is probably Minerva Stilley – she is the only woman who would remember the house in the original configuration with the back porch there. She and Frank had two sons, no daughters, so it almost has to be her.

Patrick himself had an encounter with the Lady in White on a Friday evening just before opening the restaurant for the evening. Here it is, in his very own words that he was kind enough to share with me…

Now, for my own personal experience with the "Lady in White." Friday, July 26, 1991… it was 4:45 P.M. just fifteen minutes before we opened. Just my sister and I were in the house, and she was there to wait tables. She was wearing a white blouse and black slacks. As I passed through the hall I noticed the old trunk in the hallway needed dusting. It was Louise Young's and has her name painted on the side. Her father gave it to her in 1906 when she went to college. I got the cloth and oil and got down on one knee to dust. I heard and felt footsteps coming from the Kitchen and thought it was Mary. Then the footsteps stopped in the Blue Room [now the Game Room] and crossed the hall. I looked up and saw a woman in a long white dress with puffed sleeves, and when she neared me she pulled her skirts aside, exposing high buttoned shoes. She passed me and went into the ladies' powder room, which had been an old Bedroom. I was stunned and thought, "That's sure not Mary!" I got up and went into the powder room, and there was no one there! The young woman I saw was not foggy or misty and did not float. It was a very real solid person! My next reaction was to locate my sister, and the first words out of my mouth were, "Did you just walk past me?" knowing full well she didn't. When she said, "No, why?" two customers were coming up the walk.

A few years later during Jefferson's Candlelight Tour of

Homes, a couple from the Dallas area took a picture of the Christmas lights on the neighbor's house to the east of The Grove. The next Friday they called me to say, "We're sending you a picture." Indeed, they got their photo of the Christmas lights, but in the foreground, surrounded by a "smoke ring" is a lady in a high-collared, puff-sleeved white dress!

The most recent occurrence was when a neighbor lady living a block behind us said, "Let me tell you what my sister and I have seen recently. My sister was standing on our porch one night around 9 o'clock when she called me out to see a glowing white figure across the street. She looked like she was inspecting the renovation of an old building."

When I asked the woman what it was, she said she didn't know. When I asked her where it came from, she said it came from the east side of The Grove! The lady said she and her sister had witnessed this several nights in a row, and in parting, she said, "You know, a lot of people think you're pulling their leg about that house, but we grew up right here, right behind it, and we've always known about that house!"

As for me, well, usually when I see her I'll be in the back part of the house and look up through the sheer curtains into the Game Room to see a lady walk by. My first thought is never, "A ghost!" Instead, I always think that someone is in the house.

After all, we do have a tour home, and some folks seem to think that we're open twenty-four hours a day. If we're not careful to keep things locked up, people just walk in to see The Grove. In fact, we've had folks just come in during the day and night, which as you can imagine, has made for some very interesting circumstances in our lives over the years.

But when I see her go by, I'll go up front to see that the door is locked and there's no one there, and I'll just shake my head and say, "I guess that was her again."

She showed up on the house tour one time. My wife works for the school district here in Jefferson, and she had to go represent the school at a big conference that was going on in Austin. That left me alone to get the house tour ready all by myself, and I was more than a little worried... I certainly don't have the decorative eye or touch that she has. I did my best, though, and as we went through the house, we got to the Dining Room, and I was starting to introduce the Young family. A woman stopped me and said, "I thought you said that your wife isn't home."

"She's not," I said, "she's in Austin. I talked to her this morning."

The lady nodded toward the Game Room, and said, "Then who's the lady that just walked across that next room."

"No one else is in the house," I said. After thinking about it for a minute more, I added, "Wait – what was this woman wearing?"

The lady shrugged. "I don't know. A long white dress, I think."

I couldn't help but laugh. "Wait 'til we get in there. I have quite a story for you."

That's not the only time that Minerva has shown up on the tour. One day we had a very small group, just one couple, and I went out onto the front porch to greet them.

I started the tour by telling the story of the Lady in White, and halfway through, the wife squealed and put her hands on her face.

When I asked what was wrong, her husband started laughing, and the lady told me her story.

Before I'd come outside, the lady had looked around the corner of the porch down the east side of the house and had seen a lady in a long white dress walking there. She assumed that it was the tour guide dressed in period costume, so she turned and told her husband about it. When she looked back, however, the woman had vanished... and there was no door on that side of the house.

As I was working on this book, I talked to Jodi Breckenridge, who leads the Historic Jefferson Ghost Walk every weekend, and she shared a story of the Lady in White from one of her visits.

She'd brought the group over to The Grove one evening, and had just finished telling some of the stories from the place. As they were leaving, several people said, "Who is that woman?"

They were pointing at the right side of the house, but there was no one there. Jodi asked, "What was it?" The folks replied that a lady in a long, light-colored gown with a high neck and long sleeves was walking beside the house, and about halfway down, she turned and stepped inside.

The group moved around so that they could see the east side of the house, and immediately determined that there was no doorway there. They had seen the famous Lady in White of The Grove.

Over the years people have seen her both inside of the house on the outside as well, but always taking the same path on her walk.

We have no proof that this is Minerva Stilley, but it certainly makes sense when you analyze it.

There doesn't seem to be any pattern to her appearance – it's not at any specific time of day, any season, or certainly not any specific day like Friday the 13th or Halloween. It cracks me up when people ask me about such things... I mean, do the spirits know about daylight savings time and things like that?

No, instead I've come to believe that seeing the Lady in White, like any of the other supernatural experiences at The Grove, is a right place, right time kind of thing.

Minerva probably takes her ghostly walk whether we're there to see it or not, and if we are, then all the better for us.

A Bridge-Builder:
The Rock Years, 1880-1885

One could argue that the main reason for the existence of Jefferson was a huge logjam on the Red River that predated recorded history. It was over a hundred miles long, and not only blocked the river but made it completely impassable. The logjam was called "The Great Raft," or "The Great Red River Raft."

That sent the steamboats that were looking for a passage into Texas across Caddo Lake, up the Big Cypress Bayou, and into Jefferson.

Daniel and Amanda Rock purchased the house on March 1, 1880, and according to the census records, Daniel was a bridge builder while Amanda was listed as "keeps house."

The estate of Minerva Stilley, which oversaw the guardianship to the sons John R. Stilley and Frank F. Stilley, sold The Grove to Daniel C. Rock and his wife Amanda in early 1880. The 1880 Census of Marion County gives the only clue to his identity, which is that he was a "bridge builder." One could certainly speculate that with the clearing of the "Great Raft," the depth and flow of all rivers in the area was affected, and this might be a lucrative profession at the time as rivers raised or fell to new levels. The census entry is as follows:

```
1880 Marion County Census:
Family 124
D.C. Rock (M - 43), White, Bridge Builder, Born PA
A.R. Rock (F - 29), White, Keeps House, Born IL
William Quinn (M - 29), White, Bridge Builder,
    Born IL
Maggie Quinn (F - 21), White, Keeps House, Born TN
John Quinn (M - 6), White, At Home, Born TN
```

```
William Quinn (M - 3), White, At Home, Born TN
Joseph Quinn (M - 8 mo), White, At Home, Born TN
Julian Quinn (M - 8 mo), White, At Home, Born TN
```

There is no indication as to the identity of the second family living in the home, the Quinn family, although since his occupation is also listed as being a bridge builder, he is probably an associate or employee of Daniel. Since William Quinn was born in Illinois, as was Amanda Rock, they could also be brother and sister. If this was the case, and they are the same age, they would probably be twins, and Amanda's maiden name would be Amanda R. Quinn. This is only speculation, but is certainly a possibility.

In the book *Some Early Citizens of Marion County, Texas* by Juanita Davis Cawthon (1996), there is an entry for Amanda:

Rock, Amanda R. – joined the Presbyterian Church in Jefferson, Nov. 7, 1880, from Marshall, TX; dismissed Aug. 27, 1884 (Session Minutes of Presbyterian Church, Jefferson, Texas, 1874-1906, pp 49,399); husband, Daniel C. Rock.

A Bridge Over Big Cypress Bayou (author's collection)

50

To practice the trade of bridge building during their time, tradesmen would have to travel to the site where the bridge was to be built. Depending on the size of the job, the workers could conceivably be there for several weeks. With that in mind, it might make sense that two families shared a home (in this case the Rocks and the Quinns) so that while the husbands were away their families could share expenses and give each other comfort and security.

The Rock family must have been planning the move for some time because they sold the property in 1882 to the Burks.

While there is no indication as to the reason for the Rock family to move, one could speculate that because of his profession, the bridge-building work might have dried up. The Great Raft of the Red River had been cleared by Captain Shreve and his crews, and the Big Cypress Bayou that allowed the steamboats to service Jefferson had fallen in depth significantly. Daniel's work in the area was probably done, and he simply moved on to find other opportunities.

As you will learn in the next chapter, the Burks left the house and let it go back to the Rock family, who put it up for sale once again.

After leaving Jefferson, Daniel and Amanda ended up in Grayson County. They are buried in Hall Cemetery, west of Howe, Texas.

Something Strange: The Burks Years, 1882-1883

On September 3, 1882, the T.C. Burks family purchased The Grove and gave us the first indication that something strange was going on there.

T.C. Burks moved his family into the house, and within six months time, moved them right back out. Around Jefferson, the only explanation that he gave folks was, "We can't live there." I feel that this was the first public reporting of supernatural activity at The Grove, because by the time that the next owners purchased the house that reputation was well-known around town.

There is another clue if you look at the deed records for the house, however. When the house was sold to the fourth owners, it wasn't sold by T.C. Burks... it was sold by the second owner, the Rock family. That would indicate that Mr. Burks simply backed out of the purchase deal that he had with the Rocks, and because of that, I'd give anything for ten minutes with him to find out why.

There is no official explanation as to why the Burks reneged on the deal, only that they did not wish to live there anymore. The previous owners, Daniel and Amanda Rock, took back The Grove and lived there another three years. In 1885, the Rocks moved to Paris, Texas, in Lamar County, and sold the Grove to Charlie and Daphne Young.

Fleeing The Grove

A friend of mine here in Jefferson told me that he and his wife looked at The Grove about a year before we did. He said that the real estate agent unlocked the front door and they stepped inside.

After just a couple of steps, they both stopped dead in their tracks… the house felt ominously bad. He said that there was a foreboding, overbearing presence that just washed over him. He said that there was no doubt that they weren't welcome, and they weren't wanted there. He said that he looked over at his wife and asked, "Do you feel that?"

She nodded and replied, "Yeah… let's get out of here!"

My friend has yet to ever set foot back in The Grove, even after all of these years. I guess that he took the warning seriously.

We met another couple that was new to town just after we purchased the house. We had been invited to a local party, and since we didn't know anyone and they didn't know anyone, we ended up hooking up with them. We visited for quite a while, and they told us which house they'd bought in town, and we responded with, "We just purchased The Grove."

They looked at each other, then back at us, and hesitantly said, "You bought The Grove?"

We shrugged and answered, "Of course – we love The Grove!"

The lady said, "Oh, we looked at it, but we didn't think that it could be saved."

That confused us, and I finally asked, "What do you mean?"

"Oh yeah," she said, "the ceilings were falling down, the walls were, too, and up in the attic the rafters were cracked and broken. We thought that it was too far gone."

That didn't make any sense to me, because my father-in-law, who had a background in the carpentry and construction trade, had gone over it from top to bottom before we bought the house.

We ended up inviting them over for dinner one night, and when they walked in, the lady said, "Oh my, you have saved this house!"

It had only been a few weeks since we'd closed on the house, and we explained that we hadn't nailed a single nail yet – that we'd only been cleaning up to that point.

To this day, our friend believes that The Grove "uglied itself up" so that they wouldn't buy it.

The Grove Parlor the first day that we saw it

The photograph is from the first day that we saw The Grove. We'd called the real estate agent and set up an appointment, and I felt compelled to take a few photographs so that we could go back through them when we got home, and discuss the old house that up until then, we'd only seen from the street.

As you can tell from the picture, it presented itself much differently to us than it did to our friends!

Stories like that go on and on; it seems that any number of people looked at the house, but had something happen to quickly turn them away.

Maybe something like that happened to the Burks family, and although we'll never know for sure, it would explain their sudden departure from The Grove.

The Barber's Story:
The Young Years, 1885-1983

The fourth owners of The Grove were a couple that each had a tragic start to their life – they were born into slavery. Charlie Young was born on the Sam Smith plantation near Clarksville, Texas, and Daphne Finch was born in Natchez, Mississippi. When the Civil War ended slavery, both families moved to Jefferson.

Charlie started work as a shoeshine boy at the age of eight in Joe LePara's barber shop. When the owner noticed what a good worker he was, Charlie was taken into apprenticeship. At the age of fourteen, he was given a chair in the shop, which started his career as a barber.

Although Charlie and Daphne most certainly knew each other growing up, at some point that relationship changed, because they fell in love, got married, and on March 6, 1885, purchased the Grove to start their lives together. Mr. Charlie operated a barbershop in town just across from city hall. It had one barber chair, and the back wall was lined with ivory shaving mugs, each with a patron's name in gold letters. The names of the patrons read like a "who's who" in the city of Jefferson: lawyers, bankers, merchants and other notable men. In an article in the *Jefferson Jimplecute* on September 1, 1983, G.S. McCasland Jr. remembered that Charlie catered to the elite gentlemen of the town, and set his prices to be three times that of any barber in town to keep out the "white trash," as Mr. McCasland said.

Mr. Charlie was, according to Mr. McCasland's *Jimplecute* article, "Tall, lean and handsome, always elegantly attired in a Prince Albert coat with matching trousers and a freshly laundered white shirt with a starched collar anchored by a black bow tie. He wore highly shined patent leather shoes. In short, Charlie looked more like an ambassador from Nigeria than like a barber in a small East Texas town. And his dignified demeanor and stately manner matched every inch the grandeur of his clothes. In fact, some white folks, including myself, thought Charlie was a little 'uppity,' if not downright haughty. The only earthy, common touch about Charlie seemed to be a crude lunch pail that he carried to and from his shop each day."

Charlie Young on the Front Steps of The Grove

57

McCasland goes on to report: "One of the unusual aspects of Charlie's shop was its short working schedule: 10 AM to 4 PM, six days a week – banker's hours. At 4 PM – never later than 4:40 – he would walk to his home in the Sandtown area, lunch pail in hand, head held high, still wearing his Prince Albert coat, still looking as if he had spent the day reading diplomatic messages in some embassy instead of cutting hair and shaving beards in a barber shop."

Charlie's Barber Shop on Austin Street, Later Moody's Cafe

As to Charlie's customers, McCasland says, "It's obvious that Charlie's established clientele was virtually a 'Who's Who in Jefferson'. It's no wonder that Charlie should charge triple prices, come to work at ten in the morning and go home at four in the afternoon. The man had a lock on the town's 'blue chips'. And come to think of it, that old lunch pail that he carried was probably stuffed with a carton of Russian caviar and a flacon of Moet champagne."

Charlie was also a clarinet player, and was part of the ensemble "Hamp Walker's Colored Band." They were famous in the area – in fact, they say that a party wasn't really a party unless Hamp Walker was playing.

Daphne Young

Daphne is the one who is responsible for the gardens of The Grove. She enjoyed working out in the yard and planted beds of day lilies and tiger lilies whose descendants continue to bloom to this day.

Daylilies and tiger lilies blooming at The Grove

She reportedly loved her garden so much that she worked out there every day of the year that weather permitted.

As we were working in the garden one day, an elderly gentleman came up to visit with us. In conversation, he said that he had worked our gardens for many years; as a young boy, he was a helper to Daphne Young. He told us that they would start at one corner of the yard and spend weeks working across it. When they were finally done, they would start back at the original corner again.

The old man laughed and said, "Yeah, Miss Daphne loved her garden!"

Newspaper Ad for Charlie's Barber Shop
(A Tonsorial Artist is a Barber)

The Children

The Youngs had three kids when they lived at The Grove – a daughter named Louise, a daughter named Mabel, and a son named James.

Louise graduated high school in Jefferson and went off to Bishop College in Marshall, Texas. There she earned a degree in teaching, after which she moved back into The Grove where she would spend the rest of her life. She became a teacher in Jefferson, where she spent her entire career. Louise never married, and an older woman in town who'd known her told us that, "she was a proper, educated woman who never found a man in town that lived up to her standards." She is remembered with affection as a woman with dignified posture and quiet, courteous manner.

Mable had quite a different life; she went off to the same college and met a man who was going to become a doctor. They married, and Dr. T.E. Speed became one of the most prestigious African-American doctors in East Texas. They had a house in Jefferson on Friou Street a few blocks from The Grove and later moved to Marshall, Texas.

The third child, the son named James, was quite a mystery for a long time. We couldn't find out anything about him, and he isn't buried at Cedar Grove Cemetery in Jefferson with the rest of the family.

One day about a year after we bought the house, my wife and I were working out in the garden when we saw a sweet, elderly lady walking down Moseley Street. We'd seen her a number of times, so I told Tami, "This has to be one of our neighbors – let's go out there and introduce ourselves!"

I approached her and said, "Ma'am, I sorry to interrupt your walk, but I just wanted to say hello. My name is Mitchel Whitington and this is my wife Tami, and we purchased The Grove about a year ago."

The old woman smiled and said, "Oh, I know your house! I certainly know your house!"

Tami and I glanced at each other, and I said, "Ummm... okay, what does that mean?"

"Oh, I knew Louise Young. We grew up together."

We exchanged glances again, and then simultaneously said, "You knew Miss Louise?"

"You've got to come in," I told her. "Let's put on a pot of coffee and cut a piece of cake – we want to hear every single story that there is about the Youngs!"

She shook her head and said, "Oh, no, I won't set foot in your house."

Tami said, "But we'd love to visit with you. Why won't you come in for a visit?"

The woman's eyes got big and she said, "The haints! The haints!"

I knew that was what some of the older folks in town called spirits, so I quickly realized that she didn't want to encounter the ghosts of The Grove.

"Oh, they're not going to hurt you," I assured her. "There's nothing bad or evil in there – you probably won't even know that they're there!"

Shaking her head, she said, "I wouldn't go in back then, and I'm not going to start now."

We kept talking and ended up visiting for half an hour or more. The woman told us a lot about the Young family, and even gave us some of Louise's ghost stories. That was great for us because it confirmed that the ghost stories at The Grove go back at least a hundred years, and some of the same things that were happening to us were being experienced by the Young family as well.

At one point the lady hesitantly said, "You are aware of the family tragedy..."

We looked at each other, shrugged, and I said, "No, I don't have any idea what you're talking about."

A sad expression crossed her face, she heaved a deep sigh, and in a soft voice she said, "Back in 1908, at the age of twenty years old, the son of the family, James, took his life at the house. He hung himself on the back porch."

We later were able to verify that this tragic event did occur – James took his life by hanging on the back porch of the house. We have never been able to find out any of the surrounding circumstances, or what could lead to such a terrible end to a young life, but it does explain why he's not buried with the family. In those days suicide was looked upon as a mortal sin, and someone who took his own life could not be buried on the hallowed ground of a cemetery.

We have no idea where they buried poor James. The rest of the family is buried in Cedar Grove Cemetery in Jefferson, which is an African-American cemetery. Back then there was segregation even in death, and Charlie Young fronted the money to found the cemetery. The Young family plot is at the front gate, and we figure that since he was responsible for starting the cemetery, they got "front row seating."

As to James' remains, we've heard two stories. The first is that he was quietly buried in the Young plot there at Cedar Grove, with Charlie using his influence to put his body there even given the circumstances of the death.

The other story that we've heard is that he was buried on the property of The Grove, but we've never been able to get any concrete verification of that fact. We therefore have no idea where James' body was laid to rest.

On December 31, 1938 – New Year's Eve – Charlie Young died and was buried in Cedar Grove Cemetery. In his will, he left The Grove to his daughter Louise, who he knew would continue to take care of her mom.

Louise and her mother Daphne continued to live there for years. Daphne Young, the gardener of The Grove, died in 1955 at the age of ninety-one, having spent seventy years of her life living there.

Daphne had arrived on the property as a young bride and passed away in the company of their daughter Louise. Her funeral was held on the front porch of the house so that she could be near the flowers that she loved so much one last time. Daphne was buried beside Charlie in Cedar Grove Cemetery in Jefferson.

Louise finally retired from teaching and continued to live at The Grove. On March 27 of 1983, Miss Louise died at the age of 96, having spent her entire life at The Grove. As part of her estate, she set up a trust fund for the school, and to this day she is remembered with a scholarship given every May to a graduating senior.

Miss Louise Young

There is one curious thing about her later years; one of her friends said that when they came in to clean out the house, they found that Louise had basically moved into just a few rooms. She'd put locks on many of the interior doors as if to try to keep something out.

She also put a security light out in the garden that is still there to this day. We aren't really fans of it; the light shines in our bedroom windows, but to take it out would tear up the garden, and I suppose it does actually provide a bit of safety.

When she put it in, however, she told her friends that she had been seeing a man in a dark suit out in the garden, and she hoped that the light would keep him away at night. We assume that it's the Garden Guy that I talked about in a previous chapter.

Whatever the case, Louise was buried beside her parents in Cedar Grove Cemetery in Jefferson. Her estate put the house up for sale, and The Grove was left for the first time in almost one hundred years without a Young family member in residence.

CHARLIE'S

Barber Shop,

(Opposite Messrs. Bateman Bros.—Polk St.

Fashonable Hair Cutter and Barber.

For several years Charley Young was connected with M. J. Smith, and was a favorite with the public. He invites all his old friends to call and see him at his new stand. Sept. 12th—tf.

An Advertisement for Charlie's Barber Shop

Charlie's Return

That's not to say that a Young family member hasn't come back, however. Charlie, the barber, has come back to The Grove on a couple of occasions.

The first time that we know of him coming back, he didn't come back to see Tami or me – he came back to visit the daughter of a friend of ours.

We've known Renee for a long time, and she is a very dear friend. When we started working on The Grove, she was coming up to spend the weekend with us two or three times a month to help with the renovation.

The first time that Renee brought her daughter Kinzey with her, she was only twelve years old. Since our friend was worried that Kinzey might be afraid to spend the night in a house with ghost stories, she had a plan – she wasn't going to tell her daughter about the spirits.

We set up a small sofa in the Game Room as a bed for Kinzey, fixed up the couch in the Den for Renee, and Tami and I were in the Bedroom.

When we turned in on Friday evening, I left a couple of lamps on in case anyone got up during the night. Since we were working on the house there were ladders, buckets of paint, and so forth scattered around – we didn't want anybody tripping and hurting themselves.

On Saturday morning, I got up and was waking everyone else up to find out what they wanted for breakfast. I got Tami up, then Renee, and I finally went in and woke Kinzey up. "How'd you sleep, Kenz?" I asked.

"Pretty good," she said, "except for that man."

This immediately concerned me, since I was the only guy in the house. "Just what 'man' are you talking about?" I asked.

Tami and Renee had drifted into the room by then, as Kinzey began to describe a very distinguished African-American gentleman, with dark skin but with a white mustache and white hair.

Tami realized who she could be talking about right away, and ran to the back of the house to go through a drawer where we kept photos and papers. She returned with a photograph of

Charlie Young, the barber, and as the three of us looked at it, we realized that was exactly who Kinzey was describing.

Finally, Tami turned the photo around and showed it to Kinzey, saying, "Did he look anything like this?"

Her eyes widened, and Kinzey said, "That's the guy! He was here last night!"

The three of us exchanged glances, and I said, "Kinzey, that's Mr. Charlie, the barber. He died in the 1930s... you saw a ghost!"

"Well, it didn't look like any ghost that I've ever seen on TV," she said.

I laughed. "Of course not; but weren't you scared?"

"No," she said, "he looked as real as you or me. When I woke up, I didn't know what time it was but there were still some lights on, so I figured that maybe it wasn't that late and you guys were up front visiting with mom and that one of your friends stopped by to see how far along you were with the house. That's what he was looking at – the work that you guys are doing."

She continued, "At one point he glanced back and saw that I was awake, and he just smiled at me. I felt all warm inside like everything was all right, so I just turned over and went back to sleep."

That is a wonderful story, but I have to admit, it did make me a little jealous – after all, I'd been doing research on the Young family and documenting them for years. The fact that Charlie appeared to someone other than me hurt my feelings a little!

It happened again, though. After a tour one day, two ladies told me an incredible story. They said that since they weren't sure exactly where The Grove was located, they decided to drive by about half an hour before the tour started. As they came down Moseley Street, they slowed down to look at the house and saw that there was a man standing at the front of the garden, up by the fence. He was an old, African-American fellow, very slight of build, wearing khaki pants and a light shirt. No one was outside of the house at that time, and since I don't know the person that they were describing, it could only be one person – Charlie Young, the barber. He's only been seen a few times, and I hope that one of these days, he'll appear to me.

He did come close on one occasion, however. I was at home one afternoon doing some writing. I had my computer in the Den, and everything was quiet as I sat and worked. At the time we had our two bassets Murphy and Samantha, and they were both asleep in their dog beds just across the room from me.

Suddenly, they both jumped up, started barking, and ran to the side door. If you're a dog person, then you know that a dog has several specific barks – one for "I'm hungry," another for "I want to play," and still another for "Someone's here!" They were definitely trying to tell me that someone had arrived.

I'd heard that bark many times before, and it was such a certainty that I stood up and pulled on my shoes to go outside and find out who was there and what they wanted.

When I opened the side door, there was no one there. The dogs had seemed so insistent that I started walking around the property. I went up front, but no cars were parked up there. I looked down the east side of the house and it was clear, then walked around back to find that no one was there, either.

I thought, "Crazy dogs!" and headed back into the house. When I was approaching the back door, I glanced down at the ground and saw that resting on top of the trimmed grass was the handle to a shaving brush. I recognized what it was immediately, since I had used a shaving brush and mug for many years.

The bristles were worn off of this one and it looked very old. I looked around, but I was the only one on the property... well, except for our two bassets.

I didn't dig it out of the ground, it wasn't partially buried, it was simply resting on top of the grass that I'd mowed a hundred times... including a few days before. There could be no question, in my mind anyway, that someone had placed it there for me to find.

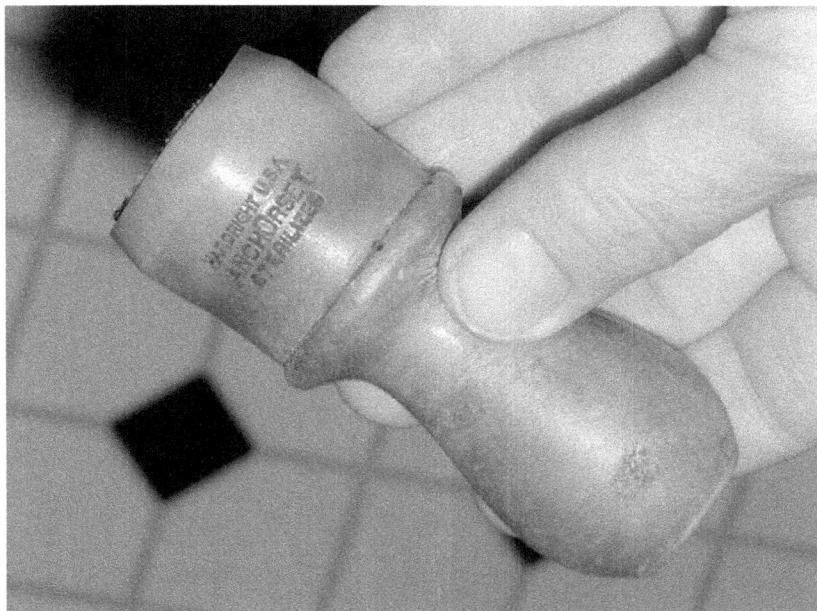

The shaving brush handle that I found at The Grove

There was a manufacturer's mark on it, so I carried the handle inside and did a quick web search – as it turns out, it was made by a shaving equipment manufacturing company back at the turn of the twentieth century.

I was wondering what it was all about, when suddenly everything fell into place. A while back, Patrick Hopkins, the former owner of The Grove, had brought us a couple of items that he found when he bought the house – Mr. Charlie's shaving mug and his mirror.

Patrick said, "I have his straight razor as well, but I have to find it. I'll bring it next time that I come for a visit. Then you'll have his complete shaving set."

A month or so went by and Patrick came by, and this time brought the razor. Just like he'd said before, "Now you have Charlie's complete set!"

As I sat at my computer holding the shaving brush, I couldn't help but grin. I think that Mr. Charlie knew that we had his mug, mirror, and razor but that we were still lacking his shaving brush. When he came back to the ghostly realm to deliver it that day, I'm sure that he was smiling and said, "*Now* you have my complete saving set!"

The Garden of The Grove, the scene of the next story

The Telephone Game

When we first bought The Grove, we heard all kind of stories about the place – and some were pretty wild. A common one was that at one point a "mad doctor" had owned the house, and he performed midnight abortions. After each procedure, he

70

would bury the fetus out in the garden beside the house where his wife planted her daylilies. This was quite a chilling legend, and we heard it more than once.

As we started researching the history of The Grove and the owners who came before us, though, the truth about the matter became clear.

Let me go back in the past – my past – for a moment. On the one and only day that I attended kindergarten, the teacher led us in a game called "telephone." All the children sat in a large circle, and the teacher whispered something in a kid's ear. He leaned over and whispered it to the next child, and so on, and so on, until the message had been passed all around the circle. When it came back to the first child, he was told to say the message aloud, and of course, it was nothing like the original – with each passing it had been altered a little.

Such was the case with the dead babies in the garden of The Grove. I believe that the story actually began in 1885 when Charlie and Daphne, and their daughter Mable married Dr. Speed .

Just like the "telephone game" story from my kindergarten days (or "day" I should say... but that's another story), we believe that the dead baby story morphed from something quite innocent.

It probably started with, "The daughter of that black family that lived at The Grove married a well-known black doctor."

As that story was relayed several times, it probably changed to, "The daughter of that family that lived at The Grove married a doctor with something unusual about him."

And from there, "A doctor with something unusual about him lived at The Grove."

At that point, it's not a far stretch to, "A mad doctor lived at The Grove."

Of course, everyone loves a good story, so... "A mad doctor who performed midnight abortions lived at The Grove."

The ultimate story finally became, "A mad doctor who performed midnight abortions lived at The Grove, and buried each fetus out in the garden among the flowers."

You see, no doctor ever lived at the place, mad or otherwise. In fact, the only doctor even associated with the house was Dr. Speed, who was a well-to-do, very respected physician. It's not hard to see how a rumor could build about The Grove over the years.

There can also be no argument that Daphne certainly kept a wonderful garden – descendents from her flowers still bloom at The Grove to this day.

The Grove Years
1983-1991

When Louise Young passed away, the property was purchased on November 9, 1983, by a couple named – interestingly enough – Colonel Daniel and Lucile Grove.

Col. Grove had already retired from a career as an Air Force Chaplin and had taken the pastorship of the First United Methodist Church in Mooringsport, Louisiana.

During a visit to Jefferson, they saw The Grove and decided that it would be a wonderful place to spend their golden years after Daniel retired from being a Methodist minister.

They started repairs to the house, even though it would be a year or so before they moved in; it had deteriorated somewhat in Louise's old age. The roof needed replacing, there was damage to the porch, and the garden was hopelessly overgrown.

Mr. and Mrs. Grove had the land around the house bushhogged and began moving some of their antiques into the small West Bedroom, where they could be locked them away until the couple could occupy the house full-time.

Tragedy struck before they could finish the house and move in. Colonel Grove was diagnosed with Binswanger's Disease, which is a rare form of dementia characterized by lesions in the brain. It is a terrible affliction, and Mrs. Grove was forced to put the house up for sale.

Before doing so, Mrs. Grove decided that she should spend at least one night in the old place. They had set up the old Master Bedroom of the house as their bedroom, even though they had never slept there.

As she lay in bed that night reading her Bible, Mrs. Grove drifted off to sleep with the light still on. She awoke to find that the room was considerably dimmer than usual, and when her eyes focused she saw that there was a dark fog slowly circling the chandelier in the room. Since it was obvious that it wasn't smoke from a fire or anything else easily explainable, she closed her eyes tightly and began to pray that everything would be okay. She awoke the next morning, with no indication that anything at all had been amiss. Mrs. Grove related that story to the next owner just before he signed the papers to buy the house. She pulled him aside before the deal was final, and said, "You should know that the house is haunted..."

Lucile isn't the only one to have seen the dark cloud, however. Patrick Hopkins, who was the next owner of The Grove, told me the story of his experience with the dark mist that happened sometime after he opened a restaurant at the house. He had organized a dedication ceremony for the garden in honor of Mrs. Daphne Young, the woman who had so lovingly planted and nurtured it. The ceremony took place in the garden, and Patrick had run back inside to the Kitchen to check on the refreshments when he found a dark cloud of smoke there. His first thought was that something was on fire, but there was no indication of anything like that. As he studied it, he saw that the "smoke" was slowly moving in a circular pattern, certainly nothing like regular smoke would do. It suddenly dissipated, and the room was clear. Patrick recalls a very positive feeling in the Kitchen and took it as a sign that the house and the spirits there were pleased with the dedication of the garden.

The next time that the dark cloud was seen, it was by a lady named Melody who spent the night in The Grove when it was a restaurant. Patrick let her and a friend stay there one evening, and she chronicled her evening in an account that she called, "One Haunted Night – A True Story." It first appeared on her personal website, but she was kind enough to allow me to use it, and so it is included in the next chapter for your consideration.

The next time that we have a record of the black mist being seen comes from a friend of ours. After we purchased The Grove, she confided to us that one evening while it was for sale and sitting empty, she and several people had sneaked inside one Halloween. She had already experienced strange things in the house, so she wouldn't go past the Front Parlor. While the other people were walking further into the house, and daring each other to go as far as the Kitchen, she sat on a windowsill in the East Parlor – the Dining Room. Someone had turned the lights on up front, so she was sitting there waiting for everyone to come back. The light suddenly dimmed in the room, and she looked up to see that the Dining Room light was enshrouded by a dark mist that was slowly moving in a circle. She yelled for everyone to come back up front, and everyone ran in to see the phenomenon. One particularly brave fellow dragged a chair over, stood on it, and stuck his hand into the cloud. She told us that the only thing that he said was, "It's freezing!" He removed his hand, and the group fled The Grove.

All of these encounters with the dark mist happened on the east side of the house – the old Master Bedroom, the Dining Room, the Kitchen, and just outside of the house.

What is this dark mist? I have no idea, even though I've seen it myself… but only once.

I was sitting in the Den – the "new room" of the house that was added by the Stilley family in 1870 – and through the sheer curtains I saw something moving across our Game Room, which was the original Master Bedroom of The Grove. It was a large, dark shape, kind of a cloud really, and it moved from the west side to the east side, blocking out the light as it went. As I watched it, I had an extremely uneasy feeling that bordered on downright fear.

As I sat there, it almost made me angry that something in the house that I loved so much had actually scared me, so I stood up and ran into that room to confront whatever was there. The room was empty – there was no black cloud or anything else. There was an electricity in the air, and I could tell that something supernatural had just passed through that room.

We have no idea what the dark cloud of mist is, or when it will show up next, although it's always somewhere on the east side of the house.

As to Mrs. Grove, well, after her husband's death she put the house up for sale, and there were several people in town that she had befriended. As they helped her clean the house out and put some of the antiques up for sale, she apparently shared a few of her experiences with them. We had more than one person tell us that they'd helped Mrs. Grove, and she quietly shared that, "A lot of strange things happen in that house."

The Grove as Patrick Hopkins Found It

The Restaurant Years
1991-2002

For a period of time, The Grove was a restaurant that was owned by Chef Patrick Hopkins who was originally from Hughes Springs, Texas.

This account is told in Mr. Hopkins' own words: *One day in 1989 I received a call from Jefferson to my office at La Camarilla Resort, Scottsdale, Arizona, asking what it would take to bring me back to East Texas. My sister mentioned an idea we had both expressed back in 1976 of opening an old-house restaurant, hopefully in Jefferson. I flew back from Arizona and scouted the Jefferson and East Texas small towns looking for that 'just right' house. After making the usual circuit in Jefferson and finding nothing new, I decided to return home and seeing Highway 59 in the distance, I thought that Moseley Street would lead right into it. Halfway down the street, I saw a beautiful Greek Revival home almost covered with vines and underbrush, with a 'For Sale' sign on it.*

Patrick knew that he had to get the house, so he contacted the real estate agent and started the process.

When Patrick was signing the papers to purchase the house and property, the previous owner, Mrs. Grove, said, "Before we sign the final papers, I think I must tell you something about the house…" She related her experience with the dark cloud there and a few other happenings, and once satisfied that she'd fulfilled her responsibility, she signed the agreement and The Grove passed to Patrick J. Hopkins.

Patrick and his sister, Mrs. Mary Hopkins Callas began the repair and restoration of the place in order to open it as a restaurant.

A contractor from Marshall was hired to do some of the work, but after a short time, his assistant quit, refusing to come back to The Grove. The contractor kept working, but finally asked Patrick, "Is this house haunted?"

Although he had already been experiencing odd things on his own, Patrick questioned the man, "Why would you ask that?"

The contractor explained: "Just before my assistant quit, I sent him out front to get something from the truck. While I was still working inside, I heard footsteps coming from the back of the house – I figured that my assistant had walked around and come in the back door for some reason. After a while, I wondered why he just standing there watching me, so I turned to ask him, but…"

"Well, who was it?" Patrick asked.

"Not who – but what. All I could say was it was like a gray, moving fog, and as it was registering to me what it was, it just disappeared!"

Thankfully, the contractor completed the work on The

Grove, although he did it alone since his assistant never came back.

The Restaurant Menu

The Grove opened with a delectable menu, along with specialty nights such as dinner theaters and an annual celebration of Thomas Jefferson's birthday.

The Grove Menu Cover

The menu described the restaurant by saying: *"Seating accommodates approximately 30-40 people in a normal restaurant setting. Current operating hours are: from 5 PM 'til..., Thurs, Friday Saturday, Sunday, and Monday. We are available for private parties and weddings. The Grove is located a mere five blocks from downtown Jefferson between Alley and Line Streets. The Grove sits amidst the Historic District. Lions Park, Secession Hall, the Cumberland Presbyterian and Christ Episcopal Churches are all within one block's walking distance. The Grove offers the convenience of today along with the serenity of yesteryear."*

Offerings on The Grove's menu included:

Homemade Soup du Jour - $2.75

The Classic Cesar Salad - $3.50
Tossed Green Salad - $2.75

Rib Eye Steak - $15.00
New York Strip - $15.00
Chicken Picatta - $15.00
Chicken Arivaca - $15.00
Seafood Market - $15.00

Swedish Meatballs with Fettucini - $9.95
Italian Style Vegetables with Fettucini - $7.95

Jefferson's Original Pecan Praline Cheesecake - $3.25
Bananas Foster - $2.75
Cherries Jubilee - $2.75

Coffee or Tea - $1.00

The restaurant received many complimentary reviews. Some of them were:

"We love your restaurant! Fabulous!!" — <u>Discover Texas</u>
*"For me, the charm of this old riverport is the pecan
cheesecake that Chef Patrick Hopkins concocts in The Grove"*
— Kent Biffle, <u>Dallas Morning News</u>

*"I almost forgot I was in a restaurant. It feels more like
I'm visiting friends here."* — <u>Kilgore News Herald</u>

*"The Grove is a great addition to the Jefferson scene.
Such a delicious dinner, and delightful evening."*
— Connie Sherley, Author, <u>A Visitor's Guide to Texas</u>

"Wonderful food! Great service!"
— Reg Durant, <u>Marshall News Messenger</u>

Diners at The Grove Restaurant

81

As soon as the restaurant opened, however, Patrick and his staff began to experience many strange things.

The waitstaff would find not only cold pockets of air in the house as they dashed about serving the customers, but they sometimes had the sensation of a force of energy passing through them – as if they had unknowingly collided with some unseen entity.

The waitresses would avoid walking through the Stairwell because there was often an uneasy feeling there, an unsettling spirit that seemed to be present. Oddly enough, the entity never bothered the waiters, who would scoff at their female counterparts when they reported the experiences.

When the restaurant closed in the evening and the staff left, Patrick Hopkins locked the front door and the house sat empty through the night. When Patrick returned the next morning, things would have been moved around in The Grove – including a mirror that hadn't fallen and broken, but instead seemed to have been lifted off the wall and carefully placed on the floor.

The Protective Spirit of The Grove

Patrick also began to hear stories about a man with a long white beard and white hair at The Grove. In fact, he was mistaken for this man on a few occasions. For example, after he had finished the restoration of the house, a local gentleman from Jefferson came by and told Patrick what a wonderful job that he'd done with The Grove. He finally said, "You do remember me, right?"

Patrick didn't remember ever seeing the man before, and so he apologetically confessed that he didn't.

The man went on the explain that he was walking by the house four years earlier, and even walked up onto the porch and peeked inside one of the front windows. He went on to say, "The house was filled with wonderful antiques, but then I saw a man with white hair and a long, white beard walk into the room carrying a pistol. I realized that I must look like a peeping tom, so I turned and ran. That must have been you, except your beard was a lot longer back then."

Patrick smiled as he told the man that the house was vacant at that time, and he was in another state working as the head chef at a restaurant.

The gentleman left, a little unsettled.

On another occasion, Patrick was supposed to meet a reporter at The Grove who was going to do a story on the restaurant. He was running a bit late, and when he pulled up in front of the house the reporter was rushing down the walkway from the front porch. She appeared to be a bit agitated, so Patrick quickly introduced himself and apologized for being late.

"So you're Patrick Hopkins?" she asked.

When he told her that he was, she said, "Then who was that in the house?"

Since he hadn't opened the restaurant yet, Patrick was confused. "What do you mean?" he asked.

The reporter said that she had arrived at The Grove, parked in front of the house, and walked up onto the front porch. She knocked on the door, but when no one answered, she opened it and walked inside.

She called Patrick's name as she walked through the house, and finally found herself back in the Kitchen – no one seemed to be there. As she walked back toward the front, a man said, "Can I help you?" He was dressed in old-fashioned clothing and had white hair and a long white beard. The reporter assumed it was Patrick, and immediately began talking to him about the restaurant.

He had a puzzled look on his face and finally said, "I don't understand what you're talking about…"

It was so strange and surreal that the reporter said, "Um, you know what, I'll call you and we'll talk later," then headed out of the front door… which is where she met Patrick on the walkway.

After telling her story, she said, "If that wasn't you, then who was it?"

Patrick just smiled as they went inside of The Grove, where he showed her that no one else was in the house.

As time went by he would occasionally hear about the man with the long, white beard, but only when no one was at the house. He came to believe that it was a protective spirit who showed up when someone came on the property and the owner wasn't home.

The Restaurant Closes

Strange things continued to happen over the years in the 1990s when the restaurant was open. Patrick eventually closed his restaurant and put the house up for sale, but one of the last weekends that he had it open, a group of ladies from the Dallas area were dining there. One of them was Leslie Knowles, a well-known psychic from that area, and she walked through the house with Patrick giving her impression of different rooms.

At one point Patrick told her that he was going to have to close the restaurant and sell The Grove. He later related that Ms. Knowles stopped, thought about it for a minute or two, and finally said, "It's going to take you a very long time to sell this house – years."

"But why?" Patrick asked her.

"Because," she said, "This house will wait and select its next owners."

Ms. Knowles must have been right because the house didn't sell for a number of years… when my wife and I purchased The Grove in 2002, and it changed our lives.

Our Time – The Whitingtons, 2002-?

This is a part of the story that won't be complete – at least, not at this writing. Its conclusion will fall to the next person to pick up a pen and continue recording the history of The Grove – the new caretakers of the property, whenever they might come along. We hope that will not be for a very, very long time.

I opened this book by explaining how my wife and I came to find The Grove and make it ours, but we didn't actually move into the house right away. As our old life in the Dallas area was winding down, we were settling into our new life in Jefferson. We drove in every weekend and spent the days working on the house or in the garden, and the evenings making friends and getting to know the city.

It seemed that with each new trip to The Grove we were being immersed more and more into the world of the supernatural – strange things were happening all the time.

One such incident happened on a Friday evening in August of 2002. We'd been away for a few days, and had just returned to The Grove. As soon as I opened the front door, the first thing that I noticed was the scent of something that smelled like paint. I knew that there hadn't been any painting inside of the house for several months, so it was a little odd, but I just dismissed the whole thing and went on.

I was carrying some groceries, so I didn't turn on any of the lights in the house – I just navigated my way through by the moonlight coming in through the windows. When I turned on the light back in the Kitchen, I noticed that there was a single, round drop of a clear, yellowish liquid on the island. I thought that it was a little strange, since there were no other drops anywhere else, and the ceiling showed no evidence of anything dripping through. I pointed it out to my wife, and she touched it and rubbed the liquid between her index finger and thumb – it was very oily. I did the same, and when I smelled it, I realized that it had the same paint-like smell that I'd noticed when I first walked inside of the house. We didn't know what to make of it, so we went back out to the car to get another load.

We still hadn't turned the lights on in the Front Parlor, and as I went back inside, something caught my eye on the east side, in the south corner – it was a piece of furniture of some kind. I called for my wife to come take a look, and when I turned on the light, we saw that it was an antique sideboard for the Dining Room. It was a beautiful piece and made a wonderful addition to the room. I knew that my parents had been in town the day before, and figured that they'd run across it somewhere and picked it up for us. I soon noticed something very odd: directly in front of the piece was a puddle of liquid about two feet across.

I wondered if it had dripped from the sideboard – although it wasn't underneath the piece, the edge of the puddle was directly below the front edge of the sideboard. The sideboard itself was perfectly dry, so I was quite puzzled as to where the puddle had come from.

I then looked up and saw that something had leaked through the ceiling, and in fact was still dripping down a little. It was amazing that none of the liquid had fallen on the sideboard – I couldn't figure out how it had kept from getting on the piece of furniture. I realized that I smelled the paint-like odor again, so I reached down and touched the puddle of liquid. It was oily and had the same scent as the drop in the Kitchen.

Since it had obviously come from the upstairs attic, I grabbed a flashlight and headed up to take a look. When I got there, I saw that a piece of paneling had fallen over, and had knocked over a gallon jug of linseed oil. I'd never noticed it before and assumed that the former owner had left it there. The jug was lying on its side in a puddle of the oil, which explained the liquid downstairs. I stood it up, then went back down to start the cleanup. As we were mopping up the oil with paper towels, I couldn't help but be amazed that the oil had come *so* close to the sideboard without even a splash getting on the furniture.

When we had the puddle cleaned up, I went back upstairs with more paper towels to take care of the mess up there. I was wiping off the gallon jug and noticed something odd – the cap was one of those that had a plastic seal around the bottom, kind of like a milk jug. The seal hadn't been broken on the cap, and on closer examination, I couldn't find any holes in the jug at all. Now, if it had been some kind of varnish or something like that, as the liquid leaked out it would become thicker and eventually seal. Linseed oil doesn't do that, though. I could find no way that the oil got out of the jug.

I called my folks, and they said that they'd put the piece of furniture in the house the day before, so it had only been there for twenty-four hours, and the puddle of linseed oil wasn't there when they moved the sideboard in.

Now, I can almost buy the fact that the entire episode was a long string of coincidences: the new piece of furniture was put in the house, and the paneling upstairs somehow fell over right after that; the paneling knocked over a jug of linseed oil that happened to be near it; that somehow the plastic of the bottle and cap expanded/contracted due to the heat or something, and half of the oil leaked out and dripped downstairs, barely missing the new piece of furniture. With all of that, though, I can't explain how a single drop was placed on the Kitchen island at the other end of the house. I don't know exactly what it means, but I've always interpreted it to be the spirits saying, "Just in case you thought the oil was a coincidence, it wasn't!"

The sideboard that the oil dripped in front of

I can't imagine what message they were trying to convey, however. While we were cleaning up the puddle downstairs, I stopped and turned around toward the center of the house. "You guys are going to have to be a lot more clear with your messages," I said to the empty room, "because I'm not smart enough to understand what this means!"

Another story about The Grove that I'd like to share is one where I really believe that the spirits of the house were protecting the place – from me! We were getting ready to go to a party one night in October. I was carrying several types of chicken wings for people to snack on: Soda Pop Cola Wings, Uncle Bubba's Bourbon Wings, and Angelic Lemon wings. You might recognize those flavors from a humor-fiction book that I wrote several years ago: *Uncle Bubba's Chicken Wing Fling*. But enough shameless self-promotion and back to the story.

I'd put the wings in the sauces to marinade the night before, then popped them in the 'fridge. We were only a couple of hours away from the start of the party, so I turned on the old oven that was left over from The Grove's restaurant days. We had only closed on the house a few months before, so we hadn't replaced it yet. I opened the oven door about twenty minutes later and found that it wasn't even warm inside. Something was wrong, and the clock was ticking.

I tried the burners on the stove, and they lit right away, which made the mystery even stranger. It then occurred to me that we'd had gas heaters installed the weekend before and that the gas had been cut off for a while in the process. I realized that there were probably two pilot lights on the appliance – one for the stovetop, and another for the oven. Knowing that I'd have to light the oven's pilot, I went to find a flashlight and a wand-type lighter.

The Stove in Question

Kneeling down in the space between the oven and the Kitchen island, I opened the small chamber under the oven, and the odor of natural gas nearly overwhelmed me. I realized that there probably weren't any modern safety controls on the old stove, and so I'd basically been venting gas into the chamber for the last twenty minutes. I could see the jet for the pilot light with the flashlight, and knew in my gut that it was a bad idea to try to light it. I laid the lighter on the shelf of the island and took one more look at the gas jet. Since we were running short on time, I couldn't help but think that perhaps if I got the lighter in there and back out again quick enough, the gas in the chamber wouldn't ignite. I remember thinking, "Man, I hope I don't blow up this house." With that, I focused the flashlight beam on the gas jet, then reached back to grab the wand lighter. It wasn't there.

I looked around quickly, but it was nowhere to be found. The island was solid, so it couldn't have fallen underneath that, and besides, I knew that I'd laid it on the shelf on the island – it only has one. I was freaking out at this point. We didn't have another lighter in the house, and any hope of us making it to the party on time was rapidly fading. My wife was in the front part of the house, so I hollered at her to ask if she'd help me search for the lighter. I heard her say, "Just re-trace your steps and you'll find where you put it down."

I sat there for a second, and then called back, "But I haven't taken any steps – I'm here on my hands and knees!"

She came in, and we turned the Kitchen upside down. We moved the stove, cleared the shelf on the island, and looked everyplace possible for the lighter. Although I knew it was futile, we quickly scanned the rest of the house as well. Finally, my wife had the idea of lighting a taper candle on the stove burner, then using it to light the oven pilot light.

It was a great idea and worked well. When I was doing that, I noticed that the smell of gas was no longer in the bottom chamber of the stove. Clearly, it dissipated in the twenty minutes or so that we were searching for the wand lighter. I was able to bake the wings and still get us to the party on time. I made a mental note to pick up another lighter the next time we were at the store.

A week or so later, we were having some friends over for dinner and my wife was opening an antique buffet in the front Dining Room where we keep dishes. In one of its cabinets, lying there on a bowl was the wand lighter that I'd placed on the Kitchen island shelf two weeks before. We rarely open that side of buffet, and in fact, probably hadn't opened that particular cabinet door for months. I can only imagine that after all these years of scaring people, the spirits finally got a scare themselves! They probably had a huge meeting with everyone who haunts The Grove there, and started off with, "We're in trouble – a real idiot has bought the house…"

But that's not the only "stove" story that I have from The Grove. We wanted to replace the old stove that was in the

Kitchen with one from the 1930s to celebrate that renovation era where Louise Young made some changes to the house.

As we were working on the place, we had all of our friends scouting for us. We told them, "Any time that you're in an antique store or junk shop, keep your eyes open for a stove from the 1930s. We don't care what make or model – in fact, we really don't even care if it works. We can always find someone to repair it, but we have to get the stove in the first place to get the ball rolling."

Time passed, and we weren't getting any leads at all, which was a bit discouraging. Finally, someone gave me the name of a store in Dallas that specialized in restoring old stoves – I realized that would be our answer!

Well, it was our answer all right. What I learned was that a stove from the 1930s, if it was in any kind of condition at all, started out at a few thousand bucks and could go up to as much as you'd care to spend, depending on what had been done to restore it.

That was so far out of our budget that I just shook my head and said, "Well, that was a dumb idea. Let's go to the appliance store and buy a stove."

Before we could do that, we got a call from a friend in Dallas who had been watching an old home being restored not far from them. Apparently they'd just moved an old stove out onto the front porch. Our friend said, "We're not sure what the story is on it, but if you want to drive over for a visit, we'll go knock on the door and find out."

We did just that, and met this couple that was restoring the beautiful old home. They were kind enough to take us through the house and show us what they were doing, and after the tour, we ended up back on the front porch.

I pointed at the old stove and asked, "So what's the story with that?"

The guy looked at it and said, "Oh, that's a 1930s Chambers stove. It was in our Kitchen when we bought the place."

"Ah," I said, "so I guess you guys are going to put it back there."

"No," he replied, "we're going to have a modern kitchen. We're not sure what to do with it."

The gears in my head started turning. I was afraid to get hopeful, but I asked, "Well, would you possibly consider selling it?"

He looked at it for a minute, and finally said, "How about a hundred bucks and you haul it away?"

I couldn't get it in the truck fast enough! We had to do some work on it, but from that point on it has worked perfectly.

The 1930s Chambers Stove

But then something strange happened concerning the stove. After a short time had passed, Patrick Hopkins, the former owner of The Grove, dropped by with a box of papers for us. It was things that belonged to Louise Young, and Patrick had found them when he was putting in his restaurant.

Patrick was giving it all to us, just as we'll be doing when we turn The Grove over to the next owners (which as I've said before, I hope is not for many, many years).

These were Louise's papers that she'd saved throughout her lifetime, and you can probably imagine what we found – financial records, letters, photos, all sorts of things. In with her papers was something that simply blew our mind.

It was an advertisement for a stove... and not just any stove, but a Chambers stove. But it wasn't just any Chambers stove... it was the same model line that we'd brought into the house, with the two doors in front, the row of controls on the upper-right front, and everything else.

I couldn't help but wonder why she'd saved the ad all those years – but if she wanted a stove like that, we're delighted to have brought one into the house for her.

That's us, with our bassets Murphy & Samantha

The Grove's Architecture

Standing on Moseley Street in front of The Grove, a visitor might guess that the architecture follows the classic Greek Revival style. Looking at the front of the house, this is certainly true. Further exploration of the structure, however, reveals the influence of another style: the French Creole Architecture.

According to the website for the National Register of Historic Places, French Creole architecture is one of the nation's three major colonial architectural traditions, and appears mainly in the Mississippi Valley. Because the region was sparsely settled at the time, very little French Creole architecture was built outside Louisiana, and today Louisiana is home to the overwhelming majority of surviving examples.

Jefferson's ties to New Orleans via the riverboat trade give the city a special Louisiana link. In fact, it has been said many

95

times that Jefferson has more in common with Louisiana than it does East Texas. While the citizens of Jefferson are devout Texans at heart, a great deal of the town's architecture reflects Louisiana style.

The man who built The Grove, W. Frank Stilley, was a cotton broker from Louisiana who traveled between the cities on riverboats. When it came time to build a house in Jefferson, he incorporated a Creole influence into the floor plan.

The website for the National Register of Historic Places describes the typical rural French Creole house as follows:

1) *Houses have generous galleries.* The Grove has not only a gallery stretching across the front of the house, but also a long, Side Gallery that was enclosed in the 1930s renovation.

2) *The Structure has a broad, spreading roofline.* The entire house, including side and front gallery, is all under a single roof.

3) *Creole floor plans tend to be asymmetrical and always lack interior hallways.* Until the Side Gallery was enclosed in the 1930s renovation, there was no hallway in The Grove, and the floor plan was a reversed ell shape.

The Creole architecture of The Grove makes it a very interesting property, since the *Louisiana Studies in Historic Preservation* states that of America's six colonial building traditions, Creole architecture is the only one actually to have evolved in America.

The Jefferson Historic Survey Project

In 1995, the Historic Jefferson Foundation commissioned a cataloging of the properties in Jefferson, Texas by the Center of Historic Architecture, Gerald D. Hines College of Architecture, University of Houston. The report was delivered in November 1995, and was an urban design research study including historical documentation of 587 contiguous sites within city limits.

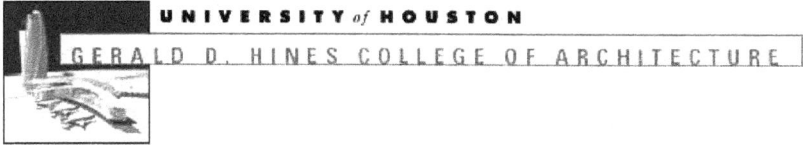

UNIVERSITY *of* **HOUSTON**

GERALD D. HINES COLLEGE OF ARCHITECTURE

During its research, the University team cataloged The Grove with the following entry:

Site Number: F092
Address: 405 Moseley
Lot: 9
Block: D
Classification: Building
Property Type: Domestic
Rating: *Contributing*

The rating of *contributing* is defined as being "a building, structure, object or site that reinforces the cultural, architectural or historical significance of the historic district."

Architectural Changes Over the Years

The outward appearance of The Grove has changed only twice in the history of the house:

1861 – The house was originally built, with a Kitchen separated from the main house.

1870 – The area between the house and the Kitchen was enclosed, which added another room to the house. This is evidenced by the fact that church bulletins from 1870 were

97

discovered in the walls of the "new" room when insulation was being added in the 1990's. Furthermore, the aforementioned 1872 Brosius Map of Jefferson shows the house with the new room, all under one roof.

1930's – After the death of Charlie Young on 12/31/1938, his daughter Louise took over the care of her mother, and of The Grove. She added a bathroom in the back of the house, removed the fireplaces from the front two rooms, and replaced the round columns on the front porch with new square columns. A well room was added behind the back porch, and the massive fireplace from the Kitchen was removed. This information was obtained through the research of Patrick Hopkins, the owner before us, and through interviews with residents of Jefferson who were acquainted with Miss Louise.

Building on the detailed research provided by Patrick Hopkins, we've spent hours combing census microfilm, Marion County records, Jefferson historical information, and first-hand interviews with the wonderful "old-timers" of Jefferson, Texas, to assemble an accurate history of The Grove. We have made every effort to preserve and maintain the original beauty of the home. The garden that was originally planted by Daphne Young is also being worked to preserve the flowerbeds that were laid out over one hundred years ago.

In 2004, The Grove was given one of the most coveted honors in the city of Jefferson: it was selected to be one of the tour homes for the city's 57th Annual Historical Pilgrimage. Along with three other homes, Oak Alley, The Claiborne House, and Sagamore, we were proud that The Grove was chosen to help represent the glorious, historical days of Jefferson to the thousands of people who flock to Pilgrimage on the first weekend in May.

During the 2005 Pilgrimage, the gardens of The Grove were included in the Jessie Allen Wise Garden Club's

"Butterfly Garden Tour." Visitors to town flocked to see the gardens that were originally planted by Mrs. Daphne Young, adorned by day lilies and tiger lilies that are descendants of the flowers that she planted a century ago.

It is our fondest wish that The Grove be a living link to Jefferson's past, and a memorial to those wonderful people who have been a part of its history.

Daphne Young's Garden – A Wonderful Place To Sit and Relax

Our Lifelines to the Future

In June, 2004 I started a simple, little electronic newsletter called the GroveZine with a couple of goals. First of all, I wanted to be able to keep people up to date who were curious about the latest supernatural occurrences at The Grove. Secondly, I wanted to chronicle the things that were happening in Jefferson as the months – and years – went by. But finally, and most importantly, I wanted to leave behind a kind of monthly diary of our time at The Grove. After all, I would absolutely love it if Charlie Young had left a series of letters about his life at the house. Unfortunately he didn't, but I can do that for the future owners.

Live From Jefferson TX...

The GroveZine!

www.thegrove-jefferson.com   December 2017   ISSN 1558-3252

"For those who believe, no proof is necessary. For those who don't believe, no proof is possible." - Stuart Chase

GREETINGS FROM THE GROVE

Hello from The Grove in Jefferson! Since this is the December GroveZine, you're probably reading it in January, but I hope that it brings back fond memories of the Christmas season for you. We had a great time here in Jefferson, from the lighting of the Enchanted Forest up in the park, to all of the different celebrations that t~-' ~' absol··' '

In the GroveZine I talk about Jefferson's happenings, things that are going on in our lives, and of course, the latest ghostly happenings at the house. I send it out free to friends of The Grove, and it started with 20 people, grew to 100, went up to 500, and before I knew it was at 1,000 subscribers. 1,500 people were getting the GroveZine before I knew it... and it keeps growing.

As excited as I am about that, the real reason that I do the GroveZine is so that future owners of The Grove will be able to sit and read about our lives here... even a hundred years from now!

As long as we're talking about a hundred years from now, something else that we did was to put a time capsule out in the yard. It's a substantial one, with room for all kinds of things.

The Author and the Time Capsule

We wanted to seal it on the 150th anniversary of The Grove – which was 2011. In preparation, I did a huge amount of research on time capsules, and found that most are buried, but more than that, when they are opened contained basically paper mâché… water invariably leaks in, and ruins everything inside.

For that reason, we decided to put it above ground, entombing it in a brick pedestal that would be opened in 2111. We did just that – and while the capsule doesn't contain anything with intrinsic value that would warrant someone breaking into it, it has many things that will be interesting a century in the future.

It has posters from all of the events in Jefferson that year, a full set of 2011 baseball cards, a set of postage stamps from the year, essays by the Jefferson High School Junior Class, and letters from many people in town. There is a Garden Club membership book, a full set of Jefferson Jimplecutes from the year, and a city phone book.

I can't even imagine who will own The Grove in the year 2111 or what the world will be like, but they will have quite a lot of historical items to go through.

The Time Capsule Column Out in the Garden

Finally, we've placed a lot of little lifelines to the future throughout The Grove. When we were doing the renovations when we first bought the house, we wrote messages on boards that we used for construction and left signatures and sentiments buried in the construction.

We've also put things in walls for future owners to discover, and to be honest, I don't even remember where they all are – but as people work on The Grove in the future, hopefully our little "Easter eggs" will provide a peek into everyday life in our time.

The Plaque on Top of the Time Capsule Column

The Investigations

Over the years that we've owned The Grove, we've had a number of paranormal investigation groups in the house, and most have come away with some incredible things. Some have not, of course, because supernatural activity is a "right place, right time" kind of thing – the spirits aren't there to entertain us or simply be at our beck and call.

Metroplex Paranormal Investigations

One of the first groups to do a full investigation of the house was Metroplex Paranormal Investigations out of the Dallas area. The team scheduled a visit to The Grove one evening in 2002, and over the course of several hours collected a good deal of interesting evidence. One of the most fascinating to me was an EVP with a voice saying "Help me…"

They were thorough and professional, and presented us with a packet containing a copy of all their findings, including photographs and recordings.

One of the most interesting things about the investigation came over a decade later, though. The psychic working with the group that evening was Dr. Rita Louise, who has become a good friend over the years.

During her initial visit, she not only picked up on the supernatural activity that we've experienced from the first but also specifics about the structure – where doors used to be, where rooms were added back in 1870, etc.

She wrote an account of her visit in her book *Dark Angels*, I highly recommend a read, by the way. It's a wonderfully insightful look at the supernatural.

Concerning The Grove, she wrote, *"Upon my first visit to The Grove I encountered no less than fifteen different ghostly anomalies. Many of these were residual. For example, when I first arrived and got out of my car, I looked up at the front porch and was greeted by one of the former (and deceased) property owners. He was dressed in brown pants and a white shirt with suspenders. He also maintained a white mustache with a full beard. He was standing in front of the front door and watched me and several members of Metroplex Paranormal Investigations as we got out of the car and started to unload our gear. I did not want to be seen as rude, so I waved to him as I made my way up the walkway to the front door. Later I learned this man is often seen standing on the porch, or just inside the front door, where he keeps watch over the house and the neighborhood.*

In the Dining Room I saw a woman. She appeared to be in her mid-twenties wearing a long blue skirt, white blouse, and an apron. Her dress gave me the impression that she had lived in the house around the turn of the century. She kept walking into the room and would tend an invisible fire in the fireplace.

In the yard, there was the presence of an older woman. I call her 'Grandma.' She could be felt along with the energy of a young girl who liked to visit with her. These are just a couple of the ghosts who live there. This list does not include the Native Americans, the secret lover and many others presences found within the bounds of their property."

As I was putting this book together, I had a conversation with Dr. Rita about The Grove, and she was kind enough to expound on some of her experiences during her first visit.

As we started talking, one of the first things that she said was, "There were all kinds of things going on at the house!"

She reiterated seeing the deceased former owner on the front porch, speaking to him as she walked by, and entering the house to pick up on the energy of a number of different spirits.

One thing that she talked about were the bodies buried on the property. In the area of the front porch she sensed that a couple had been interred with their child – not necessarily associated with the house, but from a previous time. As she stood on the porch, she looked across the garden to sense more burial plots there.

Under the house, she felt that there were Native American graves, but that these spirits were at peace. Again, they were from a time long before the house was built. She felt further Native American spirits – warriors – toward the back of the property... these, too, at peace.

One thing that Dr. Rita said was, "Oh, and the haunted mirror... I can't forget the haunted mirror!" There are actually two mirrors in the front of the house, one in the Front Parlor and the other in the Dining Room, that have strange stories associated with them.

The mirror in the Dining Room above the fireplace mantle has quite a history. When The Grove was a restaurant, owner and chef Patrick Hopkins would lock up in the evening, and then return to find the mirror on the floor – not face forward and broken, as if it had fallen off its nails, but instead propped up against the wall as if it had been carefully lifted up and set down.

Patrick also said that he would occasionally look up to see droplets of water running down the left side of the mirror. It wasn't raining outside and no moisture was dripping from the ceiling, so there was no rational explanation for the drops. He said it was if the mirror was crying.

The mirror in the Front Parlor is just as interesting. We have someone in our lives who is very sensitive to the supernatural, and while we were sitting there visiting one evening, that person became visibly disturbed. Looking in the mirror, there was apparently an image of a man, but the border of the mirror's reflection seemed to be draped in black crêpe.

When the man in the mirror was described to me, I realized that it was my father. That was a short time before prostate cancer hit him full on – he would live only for another couple of years. The black crêpe made sense because in the old days they would drape the mirrors of a home that had experienced a loss in black crêpe. It was apparently a sign that my father was approaching his death.

On another occasion, this same person looked into the mirror and saw something that was very disturbing, and not only has not shared what it was with us but will no longer sit in the Front Parlor where the mirror is in sight.

Getting back to Dr. Rita's visit, though, she said that at one point she went into the bathroom in the hallway, and had something interesting happen. Once the door was shut, she stood there for a moment, and then saw a young man walk through the door, and out a side wall. That makes sense if you know the architecture of the house – in the 1930s, Louise Young, the daughter of the Young family, enclosed the back porch on the west side of the house to make an indoor bathroom for the first time in its history. It was a very modern addition.

That bathroom was later divided into a bath and a half-bath. Looking back to the original history of The Grove, however, the porch was where James Young, the son of the Young family, took his life by hanging. If it was James he probably wasn't walking through a door and then a wall – he was most likely walking out onto the porch that was there when he was alive, and then stepping out into the garden. Since he committed suicide on that porch, he may still be walking that path.

Dr. Rita shared several other things from that night. When she walked outside to the east side of the house, she said that there was a distinct impression of a young man whose love was either jilted or unrequited by a woman in the house. After all these years his spirit apparently still lingers there.

My wife and I identified with one of the spirits that she found – the creepy guy in the Stairwell. Dr. Rita told me that when she walked past the stairs, there was a "creepy guy there."

Those are the exact same words that my wife used when we first bought The Grove. She told me, "I feel like there's some creepy guy in the Stairwell. Every time that I walk through, it feels like he's stalking me!"

Since I'd never felt anything even remotely like that, I tended to dismiss what she was saying, even though she protested.

During the first year that we lived at The Grove, we met a lady in town who'd been a waitress there when it was a restaurant in the 1990s. While discussing some of the supernatural activity that she'd experienced there, she said, "Mitchel, there's one spirit that you'll never encounter, but your wife certainly will. It's a creepy guy who hangs out in the Stairwell." My wife turned, popped me on the arm, and said, "See? I told you!"

The waitress said that none of the waiters ever had a problem, but the female waitstaff felt that this creepy guy would follow them through the Stairwell, and they'd take any other path with their food trays to avoid him. That was certainly the guy that Dr. Rita was picking up on.

My wife actually found a way to deal with him; I was in the back of the house in the Kitchen one day when I heard her yell, "WILL YOU LEAVE ME ALONE!!!" I ran to find her, and she was in the Stairwell. When I asked what had happened she said, "The creepy guy was here, so I yelled at him."

I looked around and asked, "So is he still here?"

She paused a moment and said, "I don't think so. Maybe that did it!"

From that point forward, any time that he shows up, she just yells at him and he goes away... at least, for a while.

Dr. Rita told me that after her initial walk-through, she tried to set up some video equipment in the Kitchen, but it kept losing power and freezing. We've seen that any number of times with visitors, although we have never had a single problem with batteries, electricity, etc. Still, paranormal investigators and people on the tour have had an electrical draining happen time and time again.

Wrapping up our conversation, Dr. Rita told me, "The feelings in The Grove shifted depending on where you were in the house – the Stairwell and Kitchen were kind of creepy, but the Front Parlor and Dining Room weren't bad at all." She went on to say that some of the places that she'd visited were disturbing from one end to the other, but The Grove was very different – there were many anomalies at the house. She said, "It is one of the most active locations in Jefferson, with an extended history dating long before the house was ever built, and it has an unusual number of 'visitors' who date back just as far in time."

By the way, you can find the incredible Dr. Rita Louise at www.soulhealer.com – she is a gifted psychic, bestselling author and medical intuitive.

One Haunted Night

When the house was a restaurant in the 1990s, Patrick Hopkins allowed two ladies to spend the night in the house to investigate the supernatural activity there. One of them named Melodie F. wrote her account of the evening, which she titled "One Haunted Night," and kindly allowed me to use here. This is what happened that night, in the lady's own words:

As I sat there, I watched the hairs on my arm stand up straight, one by one. I felt something I had never felt before moving through me. I felt it move up one arm, through my body and down through the other arm. At the same time, I felt a tremendous drop in temperature. Leslie grabbed her meter. I reached out my left hand and told her where to place it... the needle suddenly began jumping wildly! Any lingering doubt was suddenly and irrevocably erased from my mind. One cannot experience something such as this and walk away, still shaking their head in disbelief.

The entire night had been filled with unexpected and unexplained phenomena. This was simply the "icing on the cake" as far as I was concerned. I had entered into this endeavor with an open mind. It wasn't that I did or didn't believe in ghosts or paranormal phenomena; I guess it was more that I simply had not fully experienced them until this night.

Over the years, I had taken some photographs that, when developed, showed to have some pretty bizarre things in them. They had piqued my curiosity, to say the least, but I had no terms to attach to the weird images that had appeared in them. It was after this night's experience that I decided it was high time to make some sense out of all of it through doing some of my own research!

My friend, Leslie, had been investigating paranormal phenomena (specifically, ghosts) for a few years. During this time, she had made numerous trips to the small town of Jefferson, Texas, which is considered to be exceptionally haunted. During her visits, she met and became friends with Patrick, the owner of "The Grove" restaurant. The Grove sits away from the main streets and as you have probably guessed, is considered to be haunted.

Patrick wanted Leslie to try to spend a night in the restaurant. When her investigation partner flatly refused, she asked me if I would be interested. I jumped at the chance!

Patrick and his sister bought the property somewhere around 1990. He had to do a lot of restoration on the house before it could be made into a restaurant. It was during the restoration process that strange things began to happen and Patrick became aware that the building was haunted. According to him, objects fly through the air, sudden cold spots appear, items are rearranged, strange noises are heard... all of the things that are normally associated with a haunting.

Being away from the main portion of the town, the house sits comfortably on a back street, surrounded by trees. No other house or building stands right beside it or behind it. The street is a quiet one with hardly a car disturbing its solitude. We arrived there around 8:30 PM. We spoke to Patrick and his two waiters while we ate a wonderful dinner. They filled us in on what had happened since Leslie's last visit there. After dinner, we went for a walk. The street was dark except for the one-day-old full moon, hanging in the sky and adding to the overall atmosphere of the evening.

The Grove, photographed by Melodie

We arrived back at the house and walked around the outside of it and through the gardens. I was about to turn the corner to walk down the east side of the house when I suddenly got a very strange and spooky feeling. Mind you, I am a very logical person and I don't get spooked very easily, but this definitely caught my attention. I stopped and carefully looked down the side of the house. I saw a very large, black massive shape (had to be at least six feet tall and extremely broad)! I

111

looked very carefully to see if it could be part of the tall bushes – it wasn't. The blackness was more like a void than a shadow. I called to Leslie and asked her to look and tell me what she saw. She described the same thing that I was seeing. It was definitely NOT a human. This was one of the two things that really freaked me out during our visit. I don't know what it was, but it was not good! Did it make me uneasy? Hell, it made my skin crawl! Needless to say – I did not walk down that side of the building!

We headed back inside. Once there, we walked around the house. Leslie has a meter that checks the electromagnetic energy in an area. We took base readings around the house with it. We set up her video camera down a long hallway in the back. She uses this both for the video portion and for the sound as it is much more sensitive than a regular recorder. Later viewing only showed one slightly unusual thing. At one point there was some sort of movement that made the video camera attempt to autofocus, yet there was nothing there for it to focus on.

At one point, Leslie and I were standing just inside the entrance to the blue room (from the small hall). We both heard a noise simultaneously coming from the powder room/small hall area, and turned to look. We heard it a second time and of course, there was absolutely nothing there that we could see! What we heard sounded like the bustling of a heavily starched, (full length) skirt. As if a woman (in a bustled skirt) had just walked by. Patrick was in the small Dining Room (nowhere near where we were) and could not have made the noise. It was distinct, clear and unmistakable!

We headed up into the attic. Patrick had plans of finishing the attic and turning it into another room, but he had not worked on it for years (he really doesn't like it there!). There is no electricity up there, so we were using candles and a flashlight. There was a group of three chairs stored off in an area to the right that juts outward. I saw a shadowy figure sitting in the back chair – very plainly visible. It vanished as I watched. We set a tape recorder up in the attic but did not get anything unusual on it.

I have often heard about "cold spots" associated with hauntings, but had never experienced any... until this night. Now, I must tell you here that it was a very hot and humid East Texas night. The restaurant had two window air conditioning units for the whole place. They were not working well, and weren't cycling on very often. The temperature inside the building was around 85 degrees. Even if you stood directly in front of one of the units while it was running there was not a major drop in temperature – maybe five degrees tops.

There is an interesting photograph in the small hallway that has taken on the name of another of the houses earlier inhabitants (Minerva) despite the fact that it is not her picture. This picture dominates the wall it is on and the eyes in the picture have that rare ability to follow you around. No matter where you stand or what angle you look at the photograph from, she is staring directly at you. Needless to say, this is a bit spooky of itself!

At one point, I was standing in front of "Minerva's" picture when suddenly I felt an ice cold blast of air, like from a deep freeze, that moved through my legs. It started at the floor and went up about sixteen inches. None of the air conditioning units are even anywhere near there. There were a few other "cold spots" that I experienced but this was the most pronounced. The others varied in size and coldness yet none of them could be explained.

Patrick left about 12:30 AM. Things were fairly quiet. Other than what I have already mentioned, it was like any other night at any other house. We decided to try to get some sleep around 3 AM. Ha! (try is the operative word here!) We put sleeping bags in the middle of the entryway. There was a crystal chandelier right above us but we had it turned quite dimly. This was the only electric light that we had on since we had been using candles. We lay down to catch some shut-eye and the light started turning itself up and down... needless to say, that has a tendency to get your attention! The switch was in plain sight. No one but the two of us was anywhere near this place. The light had behaved itself quite nicely, acting like lights normally do, until the moment we laid down. When we got up, the light stopped it shenanigans... but lie back down and there it went again!

We sat up and talked for a bit. Suddenly, we heard a very loud sound, like something large and heavy had been dropped onto the hardwood floor. We both jumped and turned to look at the corner of the right Dining Room simultaneously. Of course, there was nothing out of place. We had placed a recorder on the stairs nearby. When we checked the recording later on, we heard the same loud sound so we knew it had not been our imaginations playing a trick on us.

The next thing that happened was that we began to hear car doors opening and closing outside. Now, this might not seem strange to you, but, from where we were, we could see any cars that might be anywhere in the vicinity. The only car we could see was Leslie's, and her doors were not open. This drove us a little nuts. Every time we heard a car door, we went to the window and looked out, but we never saw a thing. Being on the outskirts of such a small town, believe me when I say that there was absolutely no traffic, especially at that time of the morning. We never heard the sound of a car engine, just doors opening and closing. Leslie's car was locked tight.

A side note here on the cars – the next morning we learned something very interesting from Patrick about these car doors. Perhaps an explanation for what we heard. Apparently, back in the 20's, the house across the street had belonged to a man that had a very dastardly reputation. He was in the business of selling moonshine (bootleg, rotgut, homemade liquor). There had been rumors of lots of bad goings on there. Patrick thought the car doors that we kept hearing in the middle of the night might be tied to the man's illegal liquor trade. (i.e.: the ghost that kept arriving to get its moonshine... did something happen? Did the person never make it out of there alive? Just supposition here, but in light of what we heard, it is a possibility).

We made many trips through the restaurant that night (especially after all of the activity started). At one point, I was walking through the blue room and a movement caught my eye. I stood there and watched the chandelier swing back and forth. Leslie was in a different room, so I called her in. No, my eyes were NOT playing tricks on me... it was NOT my imagination... it WAS moving. The other chandelier in the room was perfectly still. The other chandelier was close enough to this one that whatever was making this one move should have also affected the other one...unless of course, it was being intentionally moved by unseen hands. We stood and watched it swaying for 5 – 10 min. We could not find any logical reason for the movement. The room was still and quiet. No breeze, no air conditioning, no fan. Nothing that would sway a chandelier.

Finally, being rather tired, we decided to go ahead and try to get some sleep (regardless of the antics going on in the house). Needless to say, we did not sleep much – perhaps one and a half hours total! As soon as we would drift off to sleep, there would be another loud noise of some sort (banging, bumping, etc.).

There were a few times where we had gotten into a deep enough sleep that, when we were startled awake, we were not sure exactly what we had heard. I would say that I was awakened a bare minimum of thirty times! Many of the times we were both awakened simultaneously.

On only one of these occasions did I feel really freaked out. Unfortunately, I do not know what it was that woke me. All I know is that when I woke up, I felt extremely spooked – to the point that it was all I could do to keep from jumping up and running out of the house. Now, I must reiterate here that I am not someone that really spooks easily. Believe it or not, I have too much of a logical mind for that. I wish I knew what awakened me, but I don't. I have no "earthly" (pardon the pun!) idea of what freaked me out. It took me a while to go back to sleep, but I finally did (only to be awakened quite a few more times!).

We both finally gave up on trying to sleep at about 7:30 AM. Interestingly enough, we had left the chandelier that kept dimming itself in the on position. When we finally got up, we discovered that the light had nicely been turned completely off for us!

Patrick showed back up at about 10:30 AM. He was quite surprised that we lasted through the night! We were sitting around the small table in the Dining Room when I had the most phenomenal experience of all. Patrick was sitting to my right and Leslie was getting something out of her bag.

I suddenly felt as if someone (or something) had walked right behind me, not only brushing against my back but moving THROUGH part of my back. I looked at Patrick. His eyes were huge and he said, "something is here right now." He held up his arm – he had mega goose-bumps! The "presence" moved through Patrick and back towards me. As I sat there, I watched the hairs on my arm stand up straight, one by one. I FELT something I had never felt before moving THROUGH me. I felt it move up one arm, through my body and down through the other arm. At the same time, I felt a tremendous drop in temperature. Leslie grabbed her meter. I reached out my left hand and told her where to place it...the needle suddenly began jumping wildly! Any lingering doubt was suddenly and irrevocably erased from my mind. One cannot experience something such as this and walk away, still shaking their head in disbelief.

I had felt it and the meter was going nuts! It was the strongest reading that we had gotten on the meter throughout the entire experience! When you feel something like this – it is

116

strange. You know beyond a shadow of a doubt that you have felt something. There is absolutely no question in your mind. You have touched something unlike anything you have ever touched before, and believe me – you KNOW it! It was phenomenal to have Patrick react and then the meter go bonkers! It is like having this unbelievable confirmation of something that you suddenly no longer need confirmation of! Words truly do not do it justice and cannot even begin to describe it. It is one thing to feel a cold spot here and there, to hear unexplainable noises, to have lights and chandeliers behaving abnormally, to see shapes and dark spots, but, to feel this "presence," this "thing" so very strongly and to have it verified by another person and the meter leaves no more room for doubt!

All in all, the night answered some questions for me. It made a true believer of me. Would I do it again? Well, actually I have! No, not at this same place and not under the same circumstances but I have spent the night in haunted places since and I hope to be able to continue doing so! Each place I have visited is different and unique... I chalk it up to the "Spirit" of the place!

That was Melodie F.'s account of her night at The Grove, and many people have had similar experiences.

Rahim Quazi and the Scream

I had a chance to visit with a friend of mine recently, Rahim Quazi, who's a fantastic musician. His last album was nominated for two Grammy awards, in fact. And speaking of his last album, that's one of the things we talked about. The album is

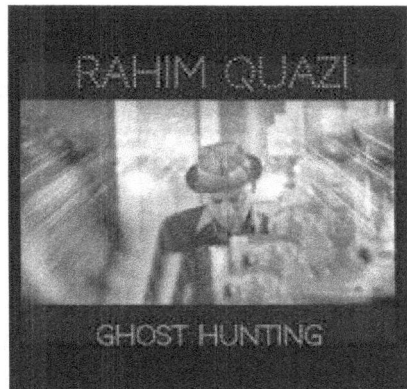

117

called "Ghost Hunting," but it's not about the supernatural – instead, it's about the interpersonal relationships that people have with each other – at least, that's my take on it. One interesting thing is that years ago before we bought The Grove, Rahim and his daughter were visiting Jefferson and came to the house. No one lived there at the time, so they were checking it out. The back door was unlocked, so they went inside and walked through the house. Rahim had a recorder with him at the time which he had running, and as they finally got to the front of the house, they heard a scream coming from the back. Of course, as freaked out as they both were, they ran out to the street. Listening to the recording later, the scream was there – captured on tape.

He kept the tape, and when he was recording his latest album, he thought that it would be fun to incorporate that scream from The Grove into the title track. He'd already recorded the music, and he was in a studio in New Orleans laying the scream over the music. When they played the scream, the recording studio suddenly went haywire – the instruments went berserk, lights were flashing, needles were pegging, and everything went crazy. There was no explanation for it – Rahim said that he hadn't seen anything like it before or since.

Things soon went back to normal, but he's never forgotten how strange that moment was. I'm just delighted that he shared it with me! He was also kind enough to put a panoramic view of the Front Parlor and Dining Room of The Grove on the interior of the CD Case.

The scream that Rahim experienced wasn't an anomaly, however. One Saturday afternoon we hosted a couple who'd been there before we purchased The Grove, back when Patrick owned it. He took them through the house, and let them return the following day. That second day when they went through the house they were standing by the front door – the house was quiet and empty, and nothing had happened to them while they were there. They were discussing that fact when there was suddenly a loud, woman's scream emanated from the back of the house, perhaps from the Kitchen.

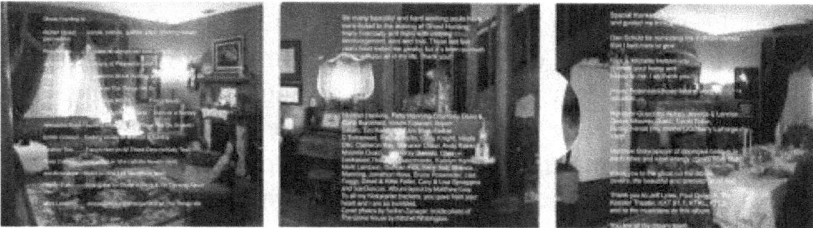

A week or so later, on our Sunday tour, one of our guests asked, "Have you ever heard a woman screaming in the house?" While we haven't had that happen, I thought that it was an incredible coincidence that it had been reported twice in a few weeks by two different people. This time, also before we purchased The Grove, the lady said that she was on the ghost walk and was standing out on Moseley Street with Jodi (the guide) when it was over, and they were talking about the spirits in the house. Suddenly, the sound of a woman screaming came from the house, and they all turned and ran.

One more story – we had some vandalism at the house one time. We woke up on a Saturday morning to discover that someone had broken our decorative mailbox off at ground level. We didn't have a clue who did it, since no other mailboxes on the street were disturbed. Our only clue was that on Friday evening Tami was calling parents to tell them that their kids didn't turn in their research papers (Tami's a teacher and a counselor). I'm sure some kids got in trouble that night, and we suspect that one of them may have taken out their frustrations on our mailbox.

I called the police when I found it, of course, and when one of Jefferson's patrolmen came out to take a look he wrote down all of the details, and then started telling me stories about

The Grove. Officer Redd has been a loved and respected member of Jefferson's Finest for years, and he was around in the years before we purchased the house. During that time when it was sitting empty, he told me that every now and then he would get a call from one of the neighbors complaining that there was the sound of a woman screaming coming from the house. Since it was usually unlocked during those days, he said that he would have to walk the entire house, including the attic, but he never found anyone there. The people reporting it were adamant, though – they swore that they'd heard the screams of a woman coming from the house.

Now, we have no idea who the screaming ghost is, but it has apparently been heard by several people – just not us! I guess that for now, the stories will just become part of the legends of The Grove.

The Night of the Orb

Now, before we get too far into a discussion of orbs, I have to say a few words. After all, "orbs" are one of the most controversial topics in the world of paranormal investigation.

By definition, orbs are circles of light that appear in photographs, usually taken with a digital camera. Since dust or moisture can easily cause these, some people dismiss all orbs as physical, explainable anomalies.

Other people capture orbs in their photographs and feel that they are the manifestation of spirits. So what is the real answer? Well, as in all things, I believe that the truth is somewhere in between. I was standing in the hallway of The Grove – formerly a side porch in the 1800s – talking on the phone, and as I was doing so a ball of light zoomed along a few inches from the floor, going between my legs as it passed.

A friend of mine was out in a field working cattle one day, and the afternoon had turned into evening. As he stood out there in the darkness, a ball of light came zooming across the field and moved over his head before disappearing into the distance.

I therefore have mixed emotions about orbs. If you want to capture some, simply walk out into a rainstorm and snap a digital photo with a flash. I promise you that you'll get hundreds of orbs in the resulting photo. Bits of dust and particles of moisture will cause orbs every single time.

On the other hand, having seen these balls of light in person and on video, I know that there is another side to the concept of "orbs."

And such is the case with a group that came to The Grove to film an investigation. They went through the house in the usual manner, taking readings and snapping photographs. Over the course of a couple of hours, they had gone through the entire house – with nothing at all happening. There were no odd readings on their equipment, no shoulder-tappings or hair-pullings, no cold spots or strange scents. It was simply a normal visit to a seemingly normal house.

The next thing that the group wanted to do was to put one of their members up in the northwest corner of the Front Parlor, alone, with a number of different cameras on him: normal, infrared, and a couple of others that I'd never heard of. Since it is the most active area of the house, they were hoping to capture some paranormal activity on tape.

They positioned the equipment, and ran wires all the way back to the Kitchen where the rest of us would sequester ourselves. A monitor was set up there with a four-way split screen so that the output from all four cameras could be viewed simultaneously. Once everything was in place, the subject was positioned in the chair in the corner of the Front Parlor – a particularly active place – and the rest of us went back to the Kitchen to wait for something to happen. But nothing did.

We stood there watching the monitor for some time, with actually no supernatural activity taking place in the Front Parlor. The folks in the Kitchen with us could talk to the subject up front by radio, and they kept checking in with him to see if he had any strange feeling that we couldn't pick up on video. There was nothing of that regard, either; he was having a very ordinary evening.

Finally, one of the guys in the Kitchen picked up a small video camera and said, "Since there's nothing going on, I'm going to at least get some footage of you guys watching the monitor." He stepped back, started recording, and suddenly exclaimed, "Oh my God! You've gotta see this!"

He ran over to us, rewinding the video, and played it back. We could see that the rest of us were crowded around the screen watching it, but the most amazing thing was happening – a ball of light was zooming in and out around us.

We didn't see it with our naked eye, but the video camera caught its movements for several minutes. Someone finally said, "Why'd you stop shooting?"

The fellow stepped back and raised the camera again. After a couple of minutes, however, it was obvious that the light anomaly had moved on – it never showed back up.

We don't know what it was, or why we couldn't see it even though it was moving in out between all of our bodies. Perhaps it was in some light spectrum that the eye couldn't detect but the camera could. Who knows – but this certainly wasn't moisture or dust in the air.

One thing for certain, however, is that it was quite a surprise. The lesson that I took away from the experience was that with the world of the supernatural, you often don't get what you're expecting – you have to be prepared for anything, not just what you're looking for.

So what does this say about orbs? Well, to me, it's like the old adage, "Don't throw the baby out with the bathwater." In other words, don't categorically eliminate something good just because you're trying to get rid of something bad. You can definitely get an orb photo by taking a flash photo with a digital camera in a rainstorm, but they can also represent something more, be it a manifestation of energy or an equally interesting anomaly.

The B.S. Visit

We got a call one day in the Spring of 2005 from a lady that we knew here in Jefferson. She told us that she'd been hired by a television production company that was filming a program about ghosts for the Showtime Network. She said that she'd told the producers about The Grove and that they wanted to film at the house. The subjects would be three paranormal investigators, who would go through the house looking for phenomena while the Showtime cameras simply filmed them.

We thought that it would be fun, so we agreed, and got ready for them to them to come to Jefferson. On Friday, March 4, the Showtime vans rolled up to The Grove and the crew unpacked to start the cameras rolling.

The three paranormal investigators prepared their equipment as well, and like any investigators worth their salt, they removed all the current batteries and replaced them with fresh, new ones.

As they began their walk through the house, one carried an EMF meter and another carried a video camera. The third was a sensitive, and was simply using her feelings to search for anything unusual. The film crew followed close behind, recording their every movement. I trailed the crew, just quietly observing.

At one point as the trio was walking up the staircase, something very dramatic happened – the EMF meter pegged, the screen of the video camera went to static, and then both instruments died simultaneously. All this was filmed, which I thought would be an exceptional addition to the program.

Before leaving the director filmed an interview with me. He had me leaning over on the railing of the front porch, with the camera on the walkway below it. I was bent over in a strange, unnatural, and uncomfortable position, but he asked me questions and had me talking about The Grove for about half an hour.

*That's me, leaning uncomfortably on the railing,
being interviewed by Showtime.*

Finally, the film crew packed away the cameras, the investigators gathered their equipment, and everyone was leaving. I asked the producer, "So, what is the name of this program on ghosts, and when will it air?"

He looked at me like he was a little confused, and said, "This is an episode of *Penn & Teller's Bullsh*t*. It'll be part of the next season." With that he turned and walked away, and I just stood there in silence.

I was very familiar with Penn & Teller's show. In that program, they basically ridicule anything and everything that is outside of the realm of classic science. I felt a sudden sinking sensation in my gut because I was sure that they will be making fun of us while showing The Grove on the program.

I also felt like we'd been duped because we'd only been told that it was a Showtime program about ghosts. I had naturally assumed that it was going to be about investigating them, not making fun of them. The words "Penn & Teller" weren't used on any of the release forms that we signed, were never mentioned by anyone on the crew, and were only spoken to me after the footage had all been captured and was safely packed away.

I sighed, and just kept thinking about that old P.T. Barnum adage, "There's no such thing as bad publicity."

When the episode was aired, in some ways it wasn't as bad as I'd feared, but in other ways, it was worse. The show didn't poke fun at The Grove, but it was merciless toward the three paranormal investigators.

The three were shown walking down Austin Street in Jefferson while Penn Jillette said something like, "Oooo, let's show them in sepia tone, and then go to slow motion." The video would switch to that, and Penn added, "Doesn't that make them look cooler?" or some such insult. This went on and on, like a school bully on the playground poking fun at kids unable to defend themselves.

When the episode got to The Grove, mercifully only a few seconds of my interview was shown. The thing that caught my attention, however, was when the staircase scene was shown – the instruments died simultaneously, and the picture then flashed to an interview with Dr. Steven Novella, Professor of Neurology, Yale School of Medicine and President of the New England Skeptical Society. He went on to say that batteries die all the time, and if you believe in aliens, then the aliens caused the battery drain; if you believe in ghosts, then the ghosts caused the battery drain, etc. He was saying that batteries eventually all run out, so this was not an abnormal experience.

What this very learned man ignored is that both instruments had brand new batteries, both pegged at the exact same time, and then both died simultaneously. I'm very sorry to Professor Novella, but that is NOT a random event... no matter what the educated doctor says. But that's how the Penn & Teller show handled everything – ridiculing the investigators and psychic without basis or merit. But don't take my word for it – watch the episode and see for yourself. It is *Penn & Teller's Bullsh*t*, Season 3, Episode 10, titled "Ghost Busters."

The Supposed Evil

A friend sent me a link to one particular website that had a listing for The Grove. It reads as follows:

~*The Grove*~ in Jefferson, Texas, is definitely the Hot Spot for ghosts but, no, the ghosts aren't friendly, they're evil. Many people were murdered there and buried in the yard. A group of friends and I visited The Grove about a week ago. It was around 11 P.M. and there was no moon but a clear sky full of bright stars. No fog in the air, I might add. Well, I was standing on the front porch when all the sudden something lifted me onto my tippy-toes and held me there. Gently it let me back down after a short while but almost every time we took a picture of someone you couldn't see them due to the apparition covering them up completely. It's a great ghost hunting place to go to but watch out! Some people come close to death when they visit.

Unlike the other sections in this chapter, I have to question whether these people actually visited the house to investigate it. My first reaction to the posting is that at 11 P.M. if she was standing on the front porch without permission, it would be the Jefferson Police Officers who would be lifting her on to her "tippy-toes." Outside of that, I have to say that the spirits who visit The Grove aren't evil. From my experience in the time that we've owned the house, I think that these spirits are former owners who are simply getting the opportunity to return for a visit. No one was murdered here, although the son of a former owner took his own life by hanging on the back porch (which is now the bathroom). There's also a fairly good chance that some of the former owners died in the house from illness or old age, but that wasn't uncommon back in the days before hospitals were ubiquitous.

Another website, www.onlyinyourstate.com, made its own attempt to describe the spirits at the house:

The historic property known as "The Grove" has been deemed the most haunted place in Jefferson and one of the most haunted in Texas altogether. The ghost stories date back to the late 1800s – none of its earlier owners were able to occupy the house for very long due to spirit infestations. Today, although still a private residence, The Grove is open to the public for tours. Among the ghosts, you'll see are a woman in a white dress, a man in the garden, and a malevolent entity in the basement. You can even hear EVP recordings captured in the house on its website.

There are any number of problems with this posting – not the least of which is that the Stilley family lived in the house for about twenty years, the Youngs for almost a hundred, and my wife and I are closing in on the Stilley's record with every year that goes by. While there is the spirit of a woman who walks through the house in a white dress and a man in a black suit in the garden, there's no guarantee that a visitor will see them. They show up when they want, not on any specific schedule. Perhaps the most interesting thing about the posting concerns the malevolent entity in the basement. You see, The Grove is a pier-and-beam house, so there is no basement. The high water table in Jefferson would make that a near impossibility even if we wanted to have one. There's no basement at The Grove, with a malevolent entity or otherwise!

I don't know where people get these stories about evil at the house – but some are very insistent. For example, when we first bought the house it had been sitting empty for a while, so we had some work to do on it. My wife and I had taken a break for lunch and were having sandwiches out on the front porch. I saw a man walking up Main Street, and he turned onto Moseley, headed in the direction of The Grove. He stopped in front of the house, and then started up the walkway. Stopping about halfway, he put up his hands and was kind of moving them around. Actually, he looked like one of those mimes doing the old "trapped in an invisible box" routine.

Anyway, I asked him if I could be of any help, and he simply replied, "I just wanted to see if the evil was still here."

My wife and I exchanged glances, and I asked, "What are you talking about?"

He said, "I came up to the house several years ago and I could feel that there was an evil presence. I just wanted to see if it was still here." After a few more gyrations with his open palms, he said, "Yes, it is. It certainly is."

I was saying, "I don't think that there's anything evil at The Grove…" when he turned and quickly walked away. Once again, Tami and I exchanged glances, and I just shrugged my shoulders and went back to eating my sandwich.

We saw another lady who was scared of the house one year when The Grove was on Jefferson's Candlelight Tour of Homes that is put on by the Historic Jefferson Foundation. Every year they invite four houses to decorate for Christmas, light every room with candles, and station a docent in period costume in each room to guide people through. I was on the front porch giving a quick introduction to the history of the house, and when one group came up I noticed that a lady that had gotten out of the car with them was standing out in the street. "Should we wait for your friend?" I asked.

One of the men shook his head and said, "No, she's afraid to come in the house. She's heard that The Grove is evil."

I explained that we'd owned the house for years and lived there without encountering anything "evil." I went on to say that a number of people had already gone through the house that evening with no unpleasant experiences, and that we routinely had friends and family over for dinner as well. No one ran out of the house screaming, or had any terrifying incidents.

"Well, she's heard some pretty bad things..." he said.

I couldn't help but smile. "Okay, but what about you guys?" I asked.

He laughed, and said, "We're not scared – we want to see the house!"

I said, "Step right up, and let me tell you a little about the house before you go inside..."

I don't know why some people believe all the hype that gets bantered around about "haunted" places. As I've said a few times already, I simply think that the veil between our world and the next is a little thinner at The Grove for some reason. It's not a bad place, nor is there anything evil present!

The Historic Jefferson Ghost Walk

One of the highlights of a trip to Jefferson, Texas is the Historic Jefferson Ghost Walk that is conducted by Jodi Breckenridge. It meets on Austin Street most weekend nights. Jodi's a friend of ours, and has been doing the tour longer than we've owned the house. In fact, the very first Ghost Walk ended up at The Grove for hors-d'oeuvres served by Chef Patrick Hopkins.

Jodi changes the ghost walk periodically so that it's always new and fresh for the people who take it, and The Grove is periodically included as part of the evening's walk through the streets of Jefferson.

Throughout the years, we've heard stories from Jodi and the folks who've taken the ghost walk. One of the most common things that people tell us is that the air around the house just "feels different." When the Ghost Walk comes to The Grove, it's usually one of the last places on the tour, so they're out front around 9:30 or so in the evening. So many people have told us that after going all over the downtown area, when they walk down Moseley Street, as soon as they get to The Grove, the air feels heavier and cooler – even on a hot, summer evening. One lady went as far as to say that she believed that she could be blindfolded and paraded up and down the streets of Jefferson, but she'd be able to pick out the exact moment that she was led in front of The Grove.

The Historic Jefferson Ghost Walk in front of The Grove

Other people have taken photographs of the house and garden, and when they got back home, have seen strange figures and other photographic anomalies that weren't visible to the naked eye.

Those who have done audio recordings during the tour have sometimes captured voices that weren't there at the time – something known as Electronic Voice Phenomenon.

130

Jodi herself has had some strange experiences at the house during her tour, and she's quick to share them with us. One of my favorites happened one evening as the Historic Jefferson Ghost Walk was wrapping up in front of The Grove. Jodi said that the people were spread out in the street listening to her and taking photographs, and she was standing on our little wooden bridge telling some of the stories about the house.

As she talked, she said that clearly one of the guys on the tour had stepped across the ditch and come up behind her, and had put his arm around her. She said that she felt his hand resting on her shoulder and the pressure of his arm on her back.

Jodi said that was thinking, "Oh, great. One of these guys has come up here and put his arm around me." She didn't want to make a big deal of it or cause a scene, so she simply shrugged that shoulder to let the guy know that his advances weren't welcome. Sure enough, she felt him move his hand and arm.

She kept talking about The Grove, but she told us that she did want to see who had done it so that she could keep an eye on him for the rest of the tour. She looked around to the left, and then to the right, and realized that she was completely alone on the bridge – no one had been there. No physical person, anyway.

That wasn't the only occasion where Jodi was physically touched by one of The Grove's spirits. On another ghost walk, she was standing on the brick steps of the walkway, with everyone in front of her facing the house. As she was talking, she felt a hand press gently but firmly into the middle of her back. It kept pressing, as if it was trying to move her off the step.

After looking back toward the house and seeing that no one was behind her, she told the group, "There is a hand on my back pushing me forward!"

131

Someone took a digital photo of her, and gasped when they saw that there was a basketball-sized ball of light behind her in the picture.

The Historic Jefferson Ghost Walk – Tami is in the dark shirt leaning against the tree

I mentioned that when the Historic Jefferson Ghost Walk was just getting started, it ended up at The Grove. Before the first walk came around, Jodi and some of the other ladies stopped by the house one evening to check things out. When they pulled up out front, they came up the walk to find that the front door was locked. The Grove was supposed to have been left open for them, so that was a bit of a surprise.

Jodi and one of the other ladies walked around the house to check the side door, which turned out to be unlocked. They went inside, and as they made their way through the place, they were laughing about being alone inside a "haunted" house.

Opening the front door, they found the other ladies on the porch screaming. Apparently the car that they came in was going berserk. The headlights were flashing on and off, and the other electrical systems of the car were acting up as well. This was long before everyone had remote controls for their automobiles – it was a car that was seemingly acting up on its own.

All the ladies looked at each other and then ran for the car. When they got inside and drove away, it seemed to be back to normal. They were more than a little apprehensive to have to go back to The Grove for the ghost walk, though.

But they did, and Jodi continues to bring the Historic Jefferson Ghost Walk down to The Grove on occasion. As she does, Jodi continues to collect stories about the house.

More than one have been about a man that people see on the property. After one tour the group was walking away, and two ladies stopped to take a photograph. A man had apparently walked from the house out to the road, and was watching them. Since he wasn't there earlier, the ladies squealed and called for Jodi to take a look, but when they turned around, the man was no longer there.

On another occasion on a different night, several people on the tour were listening to Jodi tell her stories, when they looked over to a tree on the east side of the property to see a man standing there. They described him as wearing light colored pants held up by suspenders, and wearing a long-sleeved shirt with the cuffs rolled up. Once again, when they turned to point him out to the others on the ghost walk, he had vanished.

Probably the most interesting story that Jodi tells – and the one that she finds most chilling, I'm sure – happened during the History, Haunts and Legends conference. It's a paranormal conference that happens in Jefferson every Spring and Fall, and one year there was a wine and cheese reception at The Grove in conjunction with the event. I was in the Front Parlor, Tami was in the Game Room, and our friend Lisa was in the Kitchen. Each of us were sharing stories from The Grove, and at the end, everyone attended a reception with refreshments.

In the course of things, Jodi and some of the attendees were out on the front porch. One of the ladies had a number of books that she'd purchased at the conference earlier in the day, and she was holding them under her arm.

As Jodi describes it, "A book flew across the porch at me. I thought that the ladies had tossed it at me to freak me out, and I said, 'Stop it! I'm already scared just being here!'"

The ladies looked at each other, puzzled, because no one had done anything. The book had flown across the porch on its own.

One of the ladies had a recorder and had it running the whole time, and when she played it back for everyone, there was something that gave Jodi a genuine chill.

On the recording you could hear her saying, "I'm already scared just being here!"

It was followed, however, by a voice that no one had heard in real time, but was present on the recording. It said: "You're not scared *yet!*"

Moving Furniture

Before we purchased The Grove, the previous owner Patrick Hopkins was showing us the property. It was the second time that we'd looked at it, and so we were getting serious.

He had been sharing a number of ghost stories with us, and at one point he told us of some folks who had come to the house to check it out one day. They'd made arrangements with him to get in the house, since no one would be there.

When they came back a few days later to tell Patrick what they'd found, the people had a videotape with them. They explained what had happened that night, and then played the tape for Patrick.

They arrived at the scheduled time and date, and walked around the property and then through the house checking everything out, and videotaping just in case something unusual happened. Unfortunately, nothing did. They were hoping for some supernatural activity – especially since they were recording – but The Grove was very normal.

The group finally climbed the stairs to the attic, and as they were taping upstairs, the silence of the house was suddenly broken by the sound of something heavy scraping on the floor downstairs.

They quickly ran down the staircase, and one of the heavy chairs in the Front Parlor had moved into the center of the room. They quickly looked outside to see if Patrick had come back, or if anyone else had arrived, but they were alone… not just in the house, but on the property.

Years later we had a visit from one of the people who were there on that occasion, with a videotape in hand. We watched them move about the empty house, then finally climb the stairs to the attic, and as they were looking around, we heard the heavy scraping. We watched them run downstairs and saw that the chair had moved to the center of the room. I've got to admit, it was more than a little creepy.

It's not the only time that moving furniture has been heard at The Grove, though… although it might be the only time that something actually moved.

We had a friend who was looking after the place when we first bought it, and hadn't transitioned from our home in the Dallas area to Jefferson. That friend had a key, and on several occasions told me that she'd been doing something out in the yard, when she heard heavy scraping from inside the house, as if furniture was being moved around. "Someone's inside!" she thought, and ran into the house, using the key to let her in the front door, only to find that the house was empty and nothing was disturbed.

I've had the same thing happen on any number of occasions. I've been outside the house for whatever reason, the only one on the property, and then heard the heavy scrapes of furniture moving inside the house. I used to dash inside to see what was going on, but I'd find that nothing was disturbed at all. Nowadays I just shrug my shoulders and go on with whatever I'm doing outside. I don't understand what's causing the noise, but unlike the folks who found that the chair had moved, I've come to understand that for me, it's just an unexplainable phenomenon.

The Moratorium

Now for one more word about paranormal investigations at The Grove. At the time of this writing, we've put a moratorium on them. We have the utmost respect for paranormal investigation groups; we have close friends in the field, including the founders of many groups in the region, and we have enjoyed accompanying different groups on their outings.

There are several reasons why we currently aren't having investigations at The Grove at the moment, though:

1) There have been many investigations throughout the years, only a few of which I've talked about in this book. As I said earlier, some groups have come away empty-handed, others have captured some incredible things: EVP, spheres of light on video, and countless interesting photographs. There are first-hand reports of supernatural activity going back to the early 1900s, and reports of curious things even before that. At this point, there's just no doubt that The Grove has been the site of supernatural activity for many years, and any efforts to document that are simply redundant.

2) The number of requests to let groups investigate The Grove has grown exponentially, probably due in a large part to the ghost-hunting shows on television. We feel that if we let one group do an investigation, we'd have to let others, and

we'd be involved in it several times a month (if not every single weekend). The weekend tours consume enough of our lives right now, so we just don't have enough time to open the floodgates of investigations.

3) We've been disappointed with some of the recent investigations that have been carried out here at the house. Since we live here 24/7, we know when things tend to happen; when we've told some groups that the house is mostly active in the late afternoon, they still insist on coming over at midnight, or 2 AM, when spirits supposedly "walk the earth" or something like that. At least at The Grove, there's nothing magical about midnight, Friday the 13th, Halloween, or even June 6, 2006 (6/6/6 – when were "warned" by some folks to flee the house). None of that makes sense – we've seen the man in the garden in the morning, afternoon, at dusk, and in the evening... mostly in daylight hours, though.

There have also been some incidents where we feel like the house hasn't been respected during investigations. On the tours, we tell half history, and half ghost stories – whatever the entities are that are visiting here, our belief is that they are former owners coming back occasionally. When their stories are told, and the history of the place is treated with respect, the house seems to feel warm and pleasant. It may sound strange, but I think that the owners enjoy being remembered, and because of that they tend to be more active during those times – which may be why we've had things happen so often on the tours.

On one of the last investigations that was done here, we were told to just stay out of the way, and the group spread out over the house and grounds. A couple of investigators just ran around haphazardly snapping hundreds of digital photos in rapid succession, several dashed through the house with a meter looking for electric fields, while others were off with other pieces of equipment, all looking for hard evidence of a haunting, and to our mind, being too caught up in the "what," and not the "why" or the "who." They were disruptive, inconsiderate, and to be honest, just plain rude to the house itself. One of the members was running through the garden taking rapid-fire photos looking for "ecto," and yelled to his colleagues, "This one doesn't like me and is running away, but I'm going to get him!"

Recently, groups seem to be more concerned with "capturing evidence" than with respecting The Grove and our lives here. The request to set up cameras in every room for 24 hours springs to mind, for example.

4) Our final reason is much less tangible. After one particular investigation, the house felt, well, weird. It almost had an angry or hurt feeling, as if it was trying to communicate, "You know that we're here... why did you let those people come in and make a circus out of the place that we love so much?"

All those things, and a few more are why we aren't having any investigations right now. We've caught some grief over it, with people saying, "If you won't allow investigations, then it must not really be haunted." To be honest, we don't care whether people think that The Grove is haunted or not. The supernatural activity here has been present for a century or more, and I assume will continue to be no matter what we – or anyone else – believes. For us, though, we've learned to embrace the activity, which has become part of our family. It's an incredible affirmation that life does go on after death. We don't want the spirits exploited, tormented, and certainly not removed (one lady attempted to "cast them out and close their portals"). No matter how good the intentions of people are, we've just had some bad experiences, which have compelled us to put "investigations" on hold. To be honest, that is the case with many places here in Jefferson, for the same reasons. It's not to say that we won't in the future, but at the moment, we hope that people understand and respect our reasons.

138

The Tours

One of the things that we discovered after buying the house is that it had quite a reputation. During the restaurant years the haunted legends of The Grove had attracted the attention of the media, and so it had been in newspapers, magazines, books and on television over the years.

It was very common for us to hear a knock at the front door, and answer it to find some folks there saying, "Can we take a look at The Grove?"

Occasionally in the evening, we'd hear something outside, and look out to see a few people walking around the property. When we went outside to check it out, they'd always say, "We just wanted to see The Grove for ourselves!"

Because of this, it became apparent that to keep our sanity we needed to open the house up for regular tours – that way people could see the place, but we could control access.

There are a number of tour homes in Jefferson, and so we decided that with its rich history, The Grove would be an appropriate addition to the ranks. We started the tours back in 2004, doing one on Saturday and one on Sunday.

The Parlor Corner

When people ask me what is the most common supernatural occurrence in the house, I tell them that it's not dramatic or exciting... it's a weird feeling in the northwest corner of the Front Parlor.

When I say "weird feeling," I mean that the corner feels, well, different from the rest of the room. When it's happening – which it does several times a week – it feels like there's a cloud of heavy air there. It's a little cooler than the rest of the room, accompanied by a kind of tingly feeling.

Initially, we had an antique sewing machine that we used as a table with a lamp and several knick-knacks on it, but for the last few years we've had a chair there with a floor lamp behind it. Switching the furniture didn't seem to have any effect on the activity. It still happened – sometimes in the morning, sometimes in the evening, but most often in the afternoon.

One psychic who came to the house had an interesting explanation for it. We'd been through the house, and she'd given me a lot of interesting information. Some of the things that she said about former owners and their use of the house was validated from our own historical research, so I was impressed with her abilities.

When we got back up front and she went into the Front Parlor, she walked straight over to that corner, stood there a moment, and finally turned around. "This is the strongest point in your entire house," she said.

After another minute she added, "What I'm picking up on is a female presence. She was once the lady of the house, but she's long since passed on. The house is so important to her that she comes back quite often to visit it, and when she does, this is where she mostly spends her time."

She turned back around, standing their quietly for another minute or two, and finally said, "I'm not picking up on her connection to the corner. It could be that this is where she had her favorite chair in life, and she'd sit here and drink her tea every afternoon. Or maybe she rocked her kids here... it could even be that this is where she passed. For whatever reason, though, she's strongly attached to this corner."

We talked a bit longer before she left, and I just filed that information away in the back of my mind for future reference.

Over the years, though, we've had a number of things happen associated with that corner on the tour, reinforcing that something interesting is indeed going on there.

For example, we'd been contacted by a producer whose crew was going to be shooting a television show about the haunts in Jefferson. We set up an appointment, and they arrived and started unpacking their gear.

Not only was there a full film crew, but they also brought two paranormal investigators and a psychic. We turned the house over to them, telling them that we'd be up front if they needed anything.

The crew was filming for a few hours, and as they were finally packing up their gear, the psychic lady was kind enough to sit down in the Front Parlor with us and tell us what she'd experienced in the house.

To me, the most amazing thing that she said was, "You know, we really didn't spend any time up here. When we did our initial walk-through, we started getting activity in another part of the house, so that's where we focused our attention. But by being up front here for just a few minutes, I can tell you that the strongest point in your house is that corner." She nodded toward the corner where the activity always was.

Standing up and walking over to that corner, she stood there for a while, and finally turned around. "I'm picking up on a female presence, and although I don't know who she is, I can tell that she is very possessive of this house."

We've had more subtle things happen with that corner as well. One day we had half a dozen or so people on the tour; one guy was a very large, linebacker-looking fellow. He walked over and stood in front of the chair in that corner, and his much smaller wife was in front of him. The first ten minutes of the tour is a quick overview of Jefferson's history, and I was about halfway through it when I saw him slowly moving behind the other people, edging away from that corner. He'd left his wife behind, and I don't think that she even knew that he's abandoned her.

I finally couldn't stand it any longer – I had to know. I stopped my story and said, "I'm sorry, sir, but I simply have to ask… why are you moving around the outside of the group."

He didn't crack a smile. He simply said, "There's something weird about that corner. I couldn't stay there."

Things like that have happened any number of times on the tour – people just sometimes pick up on the fact that the corner has a certain strangeness attached to it.

One of the most interesting things associated with the corner involves the name "Rachel." I was doing a small tour one Sunday morning – just one family, in fact. It was a husband, wife, and their three girls. Before we started, the mother of the family pulled me aside and said, "My oldest daughter may react a little differently to some of your stories than the other two. She has Asperger's, and although she's very smart, she tends to focus on things in ways that our other two don't." She smiled and said, "She's a very special girl." I assured her that everything would be fine. We walked in the front door, and that oldest daughter immediately made a beeline over to the corner… and she started talking to someone. The rest of us stood there watching and listening, and it was definitely one-half of a conversation that we were hearing. She said, "Oh, for the weekend…" and then "No, my family and I…"

Her mother was standing in the entryway with me, and she finally said, "Honey, who are you talking to?"

The girl looked back and said very matter-of-factly, "I'm talking to the lady."

The mother glanced over at her husband, and then looked back at the girl. "But there's no one there!"

It seemed to confuse the child. "No, the pretty lady right here! She says that they know that she's here, but they don't know her name. It's Rachel." After another minute or two the girl turned and joined her sisters across the room.

"Honey..." the mom said, "what happened to your friend?"

Again the girl looked confused. "Didn't you see? She left!" and she pointed toward the front door. By the time the tour was over, my wife and I were both hungry and left for the local Mexican restaurant. I completely forgot to tell her about the girl's experience.

Months later Patrick Hopkins, the former owner of The Grove, stopped by for a visit. We settled into chairs in the Front Parlor, and after some basic catching up, he asked the same question that he always did: "So what kind of things have been happening at The Grove lately?"

Tami said, "Well, we're not sure exactly who it is, but a woman told us that our lady in the corner over there is named Rachel!"

I added, "That's right," but turning to my wife I said, "It wasn't a woman, though. It was that girl on the tour I did, remember?"

She looked puzzled. "No, it was that woman when we had the wine and cheese event for Jodi."

I shook my head. "You're confused. It was..."

Patrick interrupted me, holding up both hands, saying, "Whoa, whoa, wait a minute. We need to explore this a little more. Tami, you go first – tell me your story."

"This happened at a wine and cheese social that we had for Jodi Breckenridge during one of her History, Haunts and Legends conferences here in town. When the lectures were over, and before the investigations that night, we had a special event for the conference VIPs. They came to The Grove and we broke them into three groups of about ten people each. We had a friend helping, and each group started in a different part of the house to hear some of our ghost stories. After they had rotated through the house, we ended up serving wine and cheese while everyone visited for a while. As the crowd was thinning out, I was up in the Front Parlor when a lady pulled me aside and said that she had something to tell me. She said that some time ago she'd lost her son in a car accident, and during the grieving process, he had appeared to her. From that point forward she said that her life had changed – she had a special connection to the 'other side.' While she was in the Front Parlor, she saw a lady standing in the corner. The woman said, 'They know that I am here, but they do not know my name. Please tell them that it's Rachel'."

Patrick nodded his head, and said, "Okay, Mitch, tell your story."

I related my tale of the family on the tour that Sunday morning several months ago. When I finished, we sat there in silence for a few moments digesting what had happened.

With a smile, Patrick said, "So each of you were given a different message, months apart, that the woman is named Rachel. That's hard to argue with."

We agreed, but unfortunately, we don't know who this "Rachel" could be. We know who all the owners of The Grove have been – even who their families were – but nowhere in the history of the house is a woman with that name. For her to continue coming back to visit The Grove, it would have to be someone who was very attached to the house. That was, and continues to be, very puzzling to us.

We have no idea who the lady is, but I sincerely appreciate the fact that she loves The Grove so much. I hope that by the time our tenure here is done – which as I keep saying, I hope is not for many more years – that we know who the spirit in the Front Parlor corner actually is!

The Queasy Feeling

The longer that we've done the tours, the more common things that we've noticed: people getting their hair pulled in the Den, folks picking up on the strange feeling in the Front Parlor, visitors even catching a glimpse of someone out of the corner of their eye, and then turning to find that no one is there.

There is one thing that has always bothered us, though, and it has manifested most frequently in the front-east area of the house – the Dining Room and the Game Room. It is a sick feeling that is experienced by guests, and when it happens, almost always by a lady. Sometimes it's a queasy stomach, other times an extreme light-headedness, but it always comes on suddenly and unexpectedly.

When I'm doing the tour in that part of the house I'm always watching our guests closely, especially the ladies. If I see anyone looking around nervously, or putting their hands to their face, or anything else that might signal that they're feeling sick, I stop telling the stories and say, "Are you okay?"

Usually one of two things will happen. Either that person will say, "No, I'm feeling a little ill," or they'll excuse themselves and head outside without saying anything. In either case, I try to get them to simply take a seat – that seems to help. If I can get the person to just sit and relax, then she can usually hang on until we move on.

Over the years, we've had a number of people actually pass out. One minute a person is standing there listening to my stories, and the next, she's falling to the floor.

On one occasion we'd put a pillow under the young lady's head, brushed her face with a wet cloth, and when she came to the guy who was with her asked, "What happened?"

She was a little confused, and said, "I don't know – I remember standing there, talking to that woman, and suddenly everything went black."

She hadn't been talking to anyone, though. She'd been standing there listening to my stories.

This continues to happen, but usually I can catch it. If a guest who's having this experience will simply sit down, when we move into the next room on the tour, the feeling will be gone.

I really don't have an explanation for it – I sometimes think that it happens because there are people who are more in

145

tune to the supernatural than they know come into a place that is so steeped in it, and they aren't prepared for the sensation.

But why does it basically only happen with ladies, and why does it seem to be restricted to the front-east corner of the house? I have no idea. I guess that it's simply another one of the mysteries of The Grove.

There was one experience that involved me – I had taken our guests into the Game Room, and I was getting ready to tell the story of Charlie Young's return for a visit. Before I got to that point, though, I saw one lady on the tour start looking very, very strange – as if something was suddenly troubling her. She was visibly bothered, and whispered something to her husband. She walked out of the room and toward the front door of the house; her husband simply said, "We have to leave," and he followed her out. I knew that something was wrong with them, and I'd give anything for her to have told me what was going on. The weird thing was, a few moments later a feeling of extreme sadness washed over me, and I felt like bursting into tears. I was in the middle of the tour, though, and I just sucked it up and kept going. The sadness was incredibly strong, and I wondered if it had hit the woman first, and then washed over me as if we were standing in the ocean and it was a wave of water. I managed to finish the tour, and that sad, distraught feeling was with me for hours – I couldn't shake it! I don't know what it was, or if it had anything to do with why that couple left the tour just before I felt it, but it was something that didn't go away for quite a while.

The D.J. and Halloween Night

This isn't something that happened on a tour, but instead after a tour was over – on Halloween.

You remember from a previous chapter about the protective spirit of The Grove – a man with white hair and a long white beard. Patrick Hopkins told me the first story about him back from the restaurant days of The Grove. A visiting gentleman had come by before the place was open for dining, and peeked in the front window. He saw an older man with a white beard coming out of the Stairwell door into the Front Parlor carrying a shotgun. The visitor ran away in fright, thinking that he'd been mistaken for a burglar. When he heard the man's story, Patrick explained that no one had been at The Grove at that time.

Patrick never saw the bearded man, since the spirit only seems to show up to protect the home. When we bought the house, in fact, Patrick told us that we'd hear many stories about him but that we'd never see him ourselves. This has turned out to be the case.

We've heard story after story about people seeing a man with a long white beard and white hair trying to frighten them away from the house. One couple brought us a photo that they took of the front door, and in the glass is a man with – you guessed it – a white beard and white hair. Where his right hand would be is a bright yellow flash, as if he was firing a gun.

I could go on for pages about this old fellow, but I want to fast-forward to something that happened back in 2006 at Mardi Gras in Jefferson. My wife and I were downtown at Sterne Fountain waiting for the Grand Parade to start, when we ran into some friends from Dallas who were in town for the festivities.

After greetings and visiting for a few minutes, the guy of the couple pulled me aside and said, "What in the world were you thinking last Halloween? Have you lost your mind?"

I was confused. "What the heck are you talking about, man?"

"What did you do last Halloween?" my friend asked.

Since it had only been a few months ago, I remembered it well. I said, "There were a lot of people in town, so we ended up having three different tours – our regular one at 2 pm, another at 4 pm, and the last at 6 pm. That last one was over about seven, and some people hung around to talk for another half-hour or so. After everyone left we shut down the house, turned off the lights, and hunkered down back in the Den to watch one of our favorite horror movies on DVD before we turned in for the evening."

He looked at me a little suspiciously. "You weren't running around your yard in costume?"

"Dude," I said, "I was so exhausted after doing three tours that Tami and I bundled up on the couch, put our feet up on the coffee table, and didn't move. And I certainly wasn't wearing a costume." I was getting more and more confused. "What in the world is all this about?"

My friend laughed and said, "I have absolutely no idea. But there's a Dallas radio show that mentioned The Grove!"

He told me the name of the program, and I recognized it immediately. "Sure," I said, "I used to listen to it back when we lived in the Metroplex."

"So you know who the sidekick on the show is, then," he said.

"'Course. I love that guy!" He was one of the cast members on the show – the one who did all of the crazy antics. "Why?"

"Well," my friend explained, "on the Friday before Halloween weekend, the folks on the show decided to send the sidekick to Jefferson to look for ghosts. They got him a room at the Jefferson Hotel and everything. Apparently he had some people with him, and they hung out in the room waiting for a ghost to show up. After a while, they got bored."

"Sure – it never works like that," I said.

"Right. Anyway, they were walking around town, and ended up adding a few locals to their posse. At some point, one of the locals told them that if they were looking for ghosts, they should walk over to The Grove. Apparently they did just that, and they walked up to the house. All of the lights were off so I guess they figured that no one was home, but as they were looking around, and old man came walking around the side of the house carrying a shotgun. He had white hair and a long, white beard. I figured that it was you, and that you had a Halloween costume on. It freaked them out so much that they all ran away. I couldn't understand why you were after them with a gun, though, unless you thought that they were prowlers."

I said, "That definitely wasn't me. First of all, I don't wear a Halloween costume, 'little old man' or otherwise. Secondly, I don't even own a shotgun – or any kind of firearm, for that matter. But most important, though, I was so wiped out from three tours in a row that I was collapsed on the couch watching a movie. I couldn't have chased anyone anywhere!"

He looked puzzled. "Any idea who it could have been?"

I couldn't help but laugh. "Oh, I think I know, all right."

"You going to say something to him about it?"

Shaking my head, I said, "Nope. I don't think that I'll ever get to see him."

There's an addendum to that story, however. A couple of months later we had a lady on our tour and before we started she pulled me away from the group and said, "If you don't mind, I'd like to have a word with you and your wife after the tour. I have to apologize for something very disrespectful that I was a part of."

I told her that it wouldn't be a problem, and all tour long I wondered what she had to say.

When everyone else left after the out, Tami and I sat down with her in the Front Parlor, and she said, "I came to The Grove last Halloween night with a group of people, including some D.J. fellow from Dallas. My friend and I hooked up with them at the Jefferson Hotel, and just tagged along to see the house."

I immediately knew what she was talking about, but I didn't say anything; I just let her continue.

She said, "When we arrived at The Grove around midnight, someone else in the group started telling stories

149

about the place, and at that point one of the guys from the radio station turned around and said, 'Here's what I think of The Grove!' He then dropped his pants and mooned the house.' Suddenly, we saw an old man coming toward us carrying a shotgun – of course, everyone scattered in an absolute panic, running back towards downtown."

"I assumed that it was the owner," she continued, "and that I'd be apologizing to him when I came on the tour today. I guess that it was your dad or something. I hope that you will forgive me."

Tami and I looked at each other, smiled, and I said, "Hey, no harm done. I do have a question for you, though."

"Certainly," she said, seeming to be a little relieved that we weren't mad.

I asked, "Is there any possible way that it could have been me, dressed up like an old man?"

She looked at me for a moment, and then shook her head. "No; no way. This was a thin guy."

Now, at that point I wasn't sure whether to be insulted or not. Instead, I just looked forward to calling my friend from Dallas and telling him that we had conclusive proof that it couldn't have been me.

Meanwhile, I kind of hate that the sidekick from the radio show and the others were under the impression that the "old man" owner of The Grove chased them away – I think that they'd be much more interested in what really happened!

Odds & Ends

In writing the book, there are a few things that didn't fit into any of the existing chapters, so I thought that a simple "odds and ends" section would be a good place to lump them together. They're as interesting as any of the other stories in the book, though, so I'd hate to leave them out.

Living in a Haunted House

One of the most interesting things about living at The Grove is that so many people assume that it's something that it's not. Not even close, in fact.

You see, folks unfortunately get their ideas about what a "haunted house" is from Hollywood. They'll see *Poltergeist* and assume that it's a documentary, instead of a fanciful, fictional story that was written and produced for the sole purpose of entertaining theater-goers, and therefore making money for the studio (and actors, and directors, etc.). That said, here are my personal favorites from that genre:

My Top Ten Movies About Haunted Houses

10. The Woman in Black
9. Amityville Horror
8. Crimson Peak
7. Poltergeist
6. The Others
5. The Conjuring
4. Annabelle: Creation
3. The Shining
2. The Changeling
1. Rose Red

The thing is… they are all simply movies! All were written by humans, not based on factual evidence or investigation, but instead meant to entertain. And by that, I mean that they were done to scare the bejeebers out of you.

Some horror movies claim to be "based on a true story," but that simply means that something about the movie has some link, minor or otherwise, to reality. In the case of the *Amityville Horror*, for example, the writer crafted the story and claimed to base it on the experiences of the Lutz family. The Lutz family actually did live in the house, and the people in the book/movie are named Lutz, so the statement that it is based on a true story is accurate. But did all of those supernatural things – bleeding walls, giant floating pigs, flies filling the house like an entomology lab – actually happen? Well, all I can say is that there have been many lawsuits and even more controversies about the accuracy of the stories. Don't take my word for it – go online and do a search for yourself. A number of people have lived in the house after the Lutz family, but never observed bleeding walls or the other things from the movie.

I'm not picking on *Amityville Horror* – it was a fun, roller-coaster ride of a movie. I am simply convinced that it was as fictional as my #1 pick on the list, *Rose Red* by Stephen King.

Yet people watch these movies and treat them as training films for experiencing the supernatural. I can't tell you how many times I've had people tell me that things happen at midnight because it's the "witching hour," just like they saw in some feature film, or that the supernatural activity comes from spirits that are "trapped" and somehow can't cross over to the other side.

Folks are surprised to see that we have a relatively normal life at The Grove. I've had people say, "You guys have a TV!" or "I saw a grill outside – do you really cook out?" It's as if they are shocked to see that we're like regular people… but we are. I think that simply because we live at The Grove, some folks think that we're *The Munsters* or the *Addams Family.*

Nothing could be further from the truth. We have dinner parties for our friends, sleep in on rainy Saturday mornings, do work projects around the house, and enjoy television shows from NASCAR races to reality TV like the show *Survivor.* We just happen to have a lot of supernatural occurrences bleed into our lives, and that makes things all the more interesting.

If you want to get a picture of life at a supernatural location, scan through the archives of the GroveZine, the free little monthly ezine that I've sent out for years. You can find them all on The Grove's website.

If, on the other hand, you want to be terrified, then whip up a batch of popcorn, turn out the lights, and you have my top ten haunted house movie list to choose from!

Shadow People

During the first year that we owned The Grove I had many conversations with the former owner, Patrick Hopkins, the chef that had opened the house as a restaurant in the 1990s. I always tried to pose my questions in a vague manner so that his answers were genuine and unbiased – and it was amazing how many of our experiences mirrored his. We were getting quite a bit of shadow activity, especially in a particular room of the house. They'd dash about, as if running from one room to another, always in the peripheral, just out of your direct vision. I finally asked Patrick if he'd ever seen a strange shadow or anything like that. He smiled, an immediate look of recognition on his face, and said, "Oh yes – I call them corner people, because you usually see them in the corner of your eyes."

And so began my fascination with the phenomena commonly known as "Shadow People."

One thing that continues to fascinate me is the age-old question of why spirits manifest in so many different forms. Why is it that when we encounter one entity it will be in the form of a translucent haze, while the next might be as solid as you or I? Other specters appear to be behaving the same over and over again, as if a cosmic videotape was being forever replayed – something that most call a "residual haunting." Still another manifestation is that of a shadow that is moving, darting, dancing, almost seeming to hide and lose itself in the darkness… things that are most commonly known as "shadow people."

One of the most interesting occurrences was one night early this summer, when Tami and I were sitting in the Den watching television and doing a little work. Through the glass-paned doors, I saw something moving around in the Game Room. When I turned my head to look, I saw a shadowy form step from that room into the center Stairwell. Before I could say anything, Tami said, "Did you see those two people walk across the room in there?" I'd only seen the one, but she said that there were actually two distinct shapes that moved through the room, one in front of the other.

A few nights later there was another event; the house was very spiritually active for some reason. Tami walked down the Side Gallery, then through the Stairwell toward the Bedroom, and happened to look into the Front Parlor. There was a dark figure standing beside the settee, and it turned around to face her. Even though we're used to living in a haunted house, she still screamed! I think that she was more startled than anything. By the time I got up there, it had stepped away toward the Dining Room, and wasn't there at all when I walked that direction. The air felt very heavy, though, and full of energy – it was a very intense sensation, especially for Tami.

There are many stories about them in the house. For example, one weekend we were getting ready for a garage sale, which we were going to use to clean out the attic, and that meant that going through all of the boxes stored up there. We'd spent most of the evening upstairs, and when we finally were stopping for the evening I carried one box back upstairs and when I opened the door, there was a very powerful feeling in the attic – as if someone was there, and was very emotional. I went back downstairs, and told Tami that she had to go up to check it out. I went with her, and we both felt an intense presence there. We finally headed back down the stairs, but as Tami stepped onto the stairs she saw a shadowy figure standing on the landing. Obviously we'd stirred up something in our unpacking.

The shadow activity seems to go in cycles. We'll notice it for several weeks – especially in the area of the Stairwell – and then it will simply stop for a while. I have no idea why this is, but it seems to be the case, so we just live with it.

Animal Spirits

We've always been fond of hounds – bassets, specifically. Fred was our first one; he joined our family in 1978, and was with us until he died in his sleep in 1992 at the ripe old age of fourteen.

Murphy, another male, joined our family shortly thereafter, joined by a girl basset named Samantha. They both moved into The Grove with us when we bought the place. We had Murph until his passing in 2005, and then lost Sam the same year in September.

Our next two girls were rescues – bassets named Lilly and Delaney. They were both in need of a home, which we were more than happy to provide.

The years flew by faster than I care to contemplate, and in 2016 we lost Lilly to a stroke. Two more rescues joined our family – Deveraux, a half-beagle, half-basset (called a bagle) that was picked up in the parking lot of the Jefferson McDonald's, and Bella, a basset found roaming along Highway 49. Both had been dumped and had heartworms, but with some veterinary care, they were both healthy and spoiled in short order.

I don't mean to bore you with stories of the dogs in our lives – so far – but instead I simply wanted to provide context for a few stories that I have to tell.

When we were first buying The Grove in 2002, we were signing the papers when Patrick (the previous owner) said, "Oh, and you have a couple of yard kitties!"

We were taken a little aback, and said, "Oh, no – we're not cat people, we're dog people. In fact, we have a couple of dogs that will be moving into The Grove when we do."

He laughed, and said, "They don't belong to me; they belong to The Grove. The Grove has always had cats."

Since we were animal lovers and couldn't ignore our new feline wards, we took care of them. When I came to the realization that they were killing mice and snakes on the property, however, I became big fans of the cats named Bubba and Sister.

They were both already getting up there in age, so after a few years, Bubba and Sister had passed on. It wasn't anytime at all until two more cats showed up – it was if they came to report for duty at The Grove.

This new pair, Daphne, and Elsie, became a part of the family along with our dogs. As the years went by, these weren't the only animals that we saw at The Grove.

The thing is, the others weren't actually living dogs and cats – they were spirits. That's right… but ghostly pets? Who could imagine such a thing? Certainly not I. That is, of course, until our mischievous basset hound "Fred" began paying us an occasional visit after his death.

Losing Fred was the saddest day of my life up to that point. He'd been a part of our family for fourteen years. During that time we'd changed careers, moved into different homes, downsized, upsized, and evolved like most families do over a decade or so. Through it all, Fred accepted whatever came our way, perfectly delighted just to be with us. He was the happiest basset on the planet and brought unending joy to our lives. We loved that dog.

As Fred got older, we had a few bouts with illness but were always able to pull him through with love, prayer and attention from one of the best veterinarians on Earth. A time came, though, that he became older and slower, and when he fell dreadfully ill one spring we were afraid that the end was near. It was something that we were hesitant to even verbalize between us, but we knew what might lay ahead. He was having trouble breathing, and although the vet was doing everything humanly possible, Fred was going down fast. Things were looking grim, and the doctor said that it was almost time to make a decision. My wife and I each took a day off from work to spend with Fred, holding him, helping him get around a little easier, and knowing that we were about to lose our baby.

The day before we were going to have to make that final ride to the vet, Fred made the decision for us. I came home to find him in his favorite sleeping place, looking as peaceful as if he were just taking an afternoon snooze. But he was gone.

We grieved like I didn't know possible. I literally cried until my eyes ached and there wasn't another tear left in me. We held each other, looked at photos that my wife and I had taken of him through the years, and wept again as we were putting his collar away and heard the tinkling of his dog tags one last time.

As any animal lover knows, you can never replace a pet. I once heard someone say, "Life is made of meetings and partings; that is the way of things." A year after we'd parted with Fred, we were blessed with two additions to our family: Murphy and Samantha, two bassets each in need of a home. We met up with them separately, under completely different circumstances, but knew that they were supposed to come into our lives.

Shortly after Murphy had arrived, my wife woke me up from a sound sleep. "Fred was just here!" she said, almost too excited for words.

"What?" I said in a haze, still trying to wake up.

"Fred – he was right here!" She went on to explain that she'd been feeling guilty over Murphy joining the family, as if we might be trying to simply fill the void that Fred's death left in our lives. While lying in bed asleep, she heard the jingle of dog tags and looked over to see what Murphy, who was only six weeks old at the time, was doing. There at the door to our bedroom was Fred, and she said that she had an overwhelming feeling as if he was saying, "Everything's okay, Mom. I'm fine, and I'm thrilled with the new puppy." With that he wagged his tail, turned around, and walked out of the room.

I explained to her that it didn't take a first year psychology student to understand what had happened: she was feeling an understandable guilt, and her subconscious mind had generated a dream to help her resolve the issue. My wife just looked at me and said, "Whether it was in a dream or it physically happened, that was Fred coming back to comfort me." No matter how I tried to rationalize it, the event was set in concrete in her mind. Fred had paid a visit.

Life went on. A year or so later, as the anniversary of Fred's death approached, I was carrying a basket of laundry from our bedroom. Of course, with two bassets in the house you were liable to find them sleeping almost anywhere, so as I walked through the doorway I noticed that one of them was sprawled out in the floor, sleeping soundly and oblivious to the rest of the world. I stepped over it and continued into the living room, where I noticed Murphy and Samantha both curled up on the couch. I ran back, still carrying the laundry basket, to see what I'd stepped over – but there was nothing in the doorway.

As I stopped and thought about it, I had assumed that it was Murphy lying there because I'd seen a brown and white head on the dog, something that he and Fred had in common.

This wasn't an apparition that I'd seen, it was a basset hound, and I literally stepped over it like I was used to doing several times a day. I suddenly felt very warm and secure – Fred had been there, if only for a moment. He'd been relaxing in one of his favorite spots, the entry to our bedroom.

More years rolled by, and as we were moving to The Grove my wife asked me if I thought that Fred would be able to find us, should he decide to pay another visit. I just shrugged, and as we were making the final trip out to the rental truck I turned back to the empty house. "Fred," I said a little hesitantly, "We're moving, and won't be here anymore. We'd love to have you look in on us and let us know you're okay, but we're worried that you won't be able to find us. Come with us if you can." There was nothing but silence, so I pulled the front door to and locked it one last time.

The winter after we'd moved to The Grove we were sitting in the Front Parlor one evening. Murphy and Samantha were curled up on blankets fast asleep, my wife was sitting on the couch getting caught up on some work, and I was at my desk writing. A familiar, unmistakable sound suddenly broke the silence – the jingle of dog tags, with the exact sound that they'd make when Fred would shake his head when he woke up. We'd heard it a thousand times when he was alive, and there was no mistaking it that night. "Fred's here," my wife observed, and we both just smiled and went back to what we were doing, delighted that he'd made the trip with us.

My wife and I both have Cherokee ancestry, and the idea of animal spirits is something that is steeped in the Native American culture. Perhaps the idea of animals coming back after their death is not such a far-fetched thing.

On Christmas morning a few years later, I heard the very recognizable sound of a basset walking through the Stairwell and hall – the clicking of the nails of their large paws on the wooden floor is unmistakable. Both of the dogs that we had at the time, Lilly and Delaney, were still asleep. The paw-steps had stopped momentarily, but as I laid back down they started again, walking into the Bedroom. I sat back up, but there was nothing there, at least, that I could see. Lilly and Delaney jumped up and ran over as if they'd heard it as well. There was no mistaking what I heard, and I firmly believe that one of our former bassets had come back to The Grove on Christmas morning just to see how we were getting along since he or she moved on. I would have given anything for just a glimpse, but hearing their footsteps once again was enough. It was the best present that I received that year.

There have been times when I've actually caught a glimpse, though. Since there is a fence around The Grove property, we're able to let the dogs out several times a day to run around the yard and get some exercise. One evening I let them out just before bedtime, and as always, they came to the back door to come in one at a time. Delaney was first, followed in a few minutes by Deveraux, but Bella wasn't showing up. I finally went out into the yard to make sure that she was okay, and I saw her walking across the yard in the light of the streetlight that is in our garden... and she was being followed by another basset. My first thought was that one of the other two had come back outside, so I stepped up onto the back porch to see if I'd left the door open, which I hadn't. I opened it and saw Delaney and Deveraux standing inside, and my next thought was, "There's another dog in the yard!" I called to my wife; we both grabbed flashlights and covered the entire half-acre in just a few minutes... there was nothing – dog or otherwise – in the yard.

I thought about it as we went back inside, and couldn't help but wonder... was that possibly one of our other bassets, who had come back for a visit or a quick walk through the garden with Bella? In retrospect, I wish that I'd run across the yard to Bella and her friend, to see if was Fred, Murphy, Samantha or Lilly walking with her. That would have been so incredibly special. I can close my eyes and still see the two dogs from that night, silhouetted in the darkness by the light behind them, and it makes me smile.

Interestingly enough, we had a couple of more sightings in the next month. My wife had taken the stairs up to the attic, and she was bringing down some decorations when she looked on the landing of the staircase and saw the rear and wagging tail of a basset disappearing around the corner and heading down the stairs. She assumed that one of the dogs had followed her up, but when she rounded the corner, there wasn't a dog there. That made her curious, so when she went looking for our girls, they were all asleep in another part of the house – it couldn't have been any of them.

About a week later I was sitting in the recliner in the Den when I looked up and saw one of the bassets in the Game Room. They had walked in and rounded the corner, so I only saw their butt and tail. Glancing down at the floor I saw Delaney and Deveraux, so that meant that it had to be Bella. I was afraid that she might be getting into some mischief, so I called, "Bella – what are you doing in there?" I heard something beside the chair, and when I looked over the armrest I saw that Bella was on the floor beside me – all three dogs were accounted for. Of course, I got up and looked in the Game Room, but it was empty.

So who was that phantom basset hound that had been showing up? Well, over the course of our marriage we'd had four others before these three, so maybe one of them was coming back for a visit. I wish that whichever one it is, they'd quit just giving us glances and actually crawl up in my lap for a while. It's been a long time since I've had a chance to pet those first four babies!

A few months later we had another experience. Tami and I were in the Den watching TV, and the dogs had just been outside to romp in the yard for a while, so the door to the Dining Room and Front Parlor was open. I looked up and saw a basset running up there, and assumed that it was our Bella. I yelled, "Bella! Get back here!" and my wife said, "Is the door to the front closed?" I stood up and ran up front, but both rooms were empty, which was a little puzzling. I had definitely seen one of our dogs running up there. When I came back, I saw that all three dogs were in the Den in their dog beds, and I pointed that out to my wife. She said, "But I just saw..." I interrupted and said, "Yep, me too."

A week or so later, we were visiting with a friend and she said, "You know, when we came over around Christmas, we were sitting in the Front Parlor talking to you guys and I looked over into the Dining Room and saw a dog walk through. It was kind of a shadow, but there's no doubt that it was a dog that walked across the room and then disappeared." None of our dogs were up front at that time.

We don't know which one of our beloved bassets has been coming back over those few months, but it's kind of cool. I certainly can't deny what we've seen.

Bassets aren't the only spirit animals that we've seen at The Grove. There have been many occasions when we've seen cats when one of our two wasn't there – even up in the attic. Believe me, if a rogue feline was in the house, the dogs would certainly have alerted us. Yet we would see a cat walk by, and then when we investigated, there was nothing there.

Perhaps the most dramatic experience that I have with an animal spirit happened as result of a book that I wrote.

Back in 2005, when we'd owned The Grove for three years, I had a contract for a book called *A Ghost in My Suitcase*. The premise of the book was that I was going to visit and write about a haunted location in every state in the country. It turned out to be a more daunting task than I'd imagined – I ended up going to places ranging from the Winchester Mystery House in San Jose, California, to Gadsby's Tavern in Alexandria, Virginia... and many, many places in between.

The clock was ticking and my deadline was looming on the horizon, so I contacted my editor and explained that it

162

appeared that there would be a few places that I simply wouldn't be able to visit – the logistics wouldn't allow it. My plan B was to contact these few places and set up interviews by both email and phone.

This ended up working out very well – the owners of those places provided tons of information that included stories, interviews, photographs, and everything that you can imagine.

One of these places was Thayer's Historic Bed and Breakfast in Annandale, Minnesota. I conducted a series of interviews with the owner, a wonderful lady named Sharon. She was very generous with her time, photos, and other resources that I needed for the chapter.

The way that I was writing the book was like a haunted travel guide. In every chapter, I would put a history of the location, some of the ghost stories that had taken place there, and finally some of the amenities that a visitor could expect. With Thayer's, I asked Sharon if there was anything special that she featured at the inn. She said that she was a psychic and would often do readings for her guests.

I finished the chapter on Thayer's Historic B&B, and when the book came out I sent Sharon a complimentary copy. I never expected to ever speak to her again.

Months went by, *A Ghost in My Suitcase* was on the shelves, and I'd already moved on to a new writing project.

On Sunday of Labor Day weekend that year, we woke up and our basset hound Samantha was clearly in trauma. She was having trouble breathing, was very lethargic, and we knew that something was wrong. Something bad. I scooped her up, put her in the car, and headed for the nearest animal emergency room which was in Shreveport, Louisiana – about an hour away.

When I finally got her there, the waiting room was packed. The admin person saw that Samantha was in an emergency situation, so she told me that there was another critical patient in at the moment, but they'd get us in as soon as possible. I sat there holding her, and suddenly she went limp. Our beautiful little basset girl was gone.

It was a very sad Sunday at The Grove. My wife and I held each other and our other basset Lilly a lot. This was back when social media was in its infancy, so we didn't run out and spread the word about our loss. We just stayed in and kept to ourselves the rest of the holiday weekend.

A couple of days later Sharon from Thayer's Historic B&B contacted me, and said, "What's happened in your life? I keep getting a strong impression of you, like something bad has happened."

I told her that our basset Samantha had just died, and that it had been an extremely traumatic for Tami and me.

She said, "Ah, that explains a lot. I could tell that something very emotional had happened to you. But I could also see three dogs – three basset hounds – around you."

To my knowledge, I'd never mentioned the fact that we had dogs to her. More than that, however, Sharon had no way of knowing that Samantha was the third basset that we'd had in our marriage – we had Fred for fourteen years, and then adopted Murphy and Samantha. Murphy had died in January of that same year.

She went on to tell me more about Samantha. She said, "She wants you to know she didn't hurt physically very much, but is very glad that part is over. She misses the sunshine, but each time you think of her she feels it in her spirit heart – so although it's not the same, it is very similar and it makes 'here' all the better. Not to worry, she is working at her new job. She will stop in every now and again to check on you, so be ready for a blur of fur. She can move very fast now – she likes that part."

Sharon continued, telling me that Samantha and our other two were starting to search for a new dog for us. She said that the new addition to our family would have traits of all three of them.

A few months later, we rescued a basset named Delaney. And yes, she had traits of all our previous babies: Fred's inquisitive nature, Murphy's stubbornness, and Samantha's loving demeanor.

Looking back at that, I have no idea how she could have known that we had dogs, much less that one had just died. Perhaps our Cherokee ancestors were right, and animals do have spirits that go on. We certainly hope so – we live in hope of someday being reunited with all the dogs that we've loved.

Up in the Attic

People ask me all the time – where do the stairs in The Grove go? I tell them that The Grove always has been, and probably always will be, a one-story house.

The attic in The Grove is exactly like any one you've ever seen – rafters, insulation, air conditioning ducts, etc. The front part of it is floored for storage, and because of the pitch of the roof it is large enough that you can stand up and walk around up there.

When we bought the house, the attic was empty, but we had a lot of things to store up there: several Christmas trees, holiday decorations, wreaths, you name it. In all of the trips up and down the stairs as we were moving in, we never noticed anything strange about the attic... until we got settled in, that is.

We began to notice an occasional strange feeling on the stairs, as if someone was standing there with you. It definitely wasn't threatening – instead it was inquisitive, apprehensive, questioning. One time when my wife noticed it, she called me up to the landing, and I immediately felt what she did. She said, "I wonder who this is?" and instantly the name THOMAS came into her mind. She said it was as if she'd been hit with the word.

We don't know anyone named "Thomas," so she certainly wasn't thinking of a friend or relative, and it was strange that it was suddenly so strong in her thoughts, so we started referring to the entity by that name. I'd walk through the Stairwell and feel that apprehensive, tingly sensation and I'd tell Tami, "Well, Thomas is back for a visit!"

It was a little odd, because in reality the stairs were a new addition to the house – Patrick put them there in the early 1990s. Prior to that, you had to climb a ladder and open a door to get up there. I don't have an explanation as to how this fellow we called "Thomas" discovered the stairs that weren't there in his lifetime, but then again, none of us can be sure how things work on the other side.

I recall one time when we had a psychic visit The Grove, and she felt like she wanted to go up to the attic. She climbed the stairs, followed by her husband and me. Once she took a few steps inside, she doubled over and said, "Get me out of here!"

Her husband grabbed one arm, I took the other, and we half-carried, half-dragged her back onto the stairs. When we were back in the Front Parlor we put her in a chair to re-gain her composure. She finally said, "I can't tell you how strong a feeling I got up in the attic. There was someone up there who in life was scared, possibly hiding, and lived up there for a while."

I've been in the attic in the dead of winter when it's freezing, and in the heat of summer when the temperature is off the charts, so I can't imagine anyone living up there, but the longer we've lived at The Grove, the more stories we've collected about the attic.

For example, one evening the bassets were asleep in their dog beds in the Den, and the rest of the house was quiet; we were in the Kitchen preparing dinner. Suddenly we heard steps coming from the front of the house, and as I stepped into the hallway, it was obvious that they were coming down the stairs.

No one was there, of course, but some unseen entity had clumped down the stairs. Perhaps he caught a whiff of the steaks and baked potatoes that we were working on in the Kitchen and just came down to see if we'd set another place.

On another occasion, the former owner, Patrick Hopkins, dropped by with one of his sisters. In the course of conversation his sister asked, "Have you ever experienced anything in the attic?" I told her that we'd had some strange things happen in conjunction with the attic over the years. She proceeded to tell me that when Patrick had first purchased the house and started restoring it, something happened up there that her kids still won't talk about. Her young son and daughter wanted to help, so they were assigned to go up there and throw shingles that were stored up there out of one of the windows onto the ground below. In the course of doing this, they suddenly came running downstairs, their eyes as big as half-dollars. They wouldn't divulge what had happened up there, but they would never climb the stairs again. To this day, she said, neither of them will talk about it.

Other people have had strange experiences up there. Since Tami works for the local school district, we've occasionally hired some of her students when we've had some work to do around the house. One weekend we had two young men over helping us move some things. Tami told me that she felt Thomas in the attic during one of her trips up, but didn't say anything to the boys about it. A little later, one of the guys said, "Mrs. Whit, there's something weird up there – my whole body tingles when I go into a certain part of the attic, and it feels like someone's there!" We told him that it was just Thomas, probably checking to make sure that the work that was being done up there met with his approval. I don't think that either of the boys felt at ease until we'd finished the attic part of the work.

We've even had things happen on the tours related to the attic and stairs. During one of the tours, we'd just about finished up and everyone was back up front signing the guest book. Someone asked the question, "Earlier in the tour, was someone walking up and down the stairs?" I told them that I didn't think so, but said that I'd ask Tami if she'd been up there. I doubted that she was, of course, since during the summer it's hot as the dickens at the top of the stairs – let alone up in the attic itself. A couple of others on the tour said that they'd heard the stairs creaking during the first part of the tour as if someone had been walking up or down them. Of course, I checked with Tami, and she had been in the back of the house getting it ready for everyone to see, and hadn't been upstairs at all. The dogs were in the Bedroom, so I don't have a good explanation for what these folks heard – I just wish that I'd noticed it so that I could have investigated it to see if that feeling we call "Thomas" was there.

One final thing on the topic. After a tour one weekend, I received an email from one of our guests. She wrote: "My husband is from South America, and a lot of his family is sensitive to spirits. While standing in the Front Parlor, I felt like someone was watching us from up near the attic. I just assumed it was me being afraid of your house to start with, and never made mention of it during the tour. When we walked into the Game Room I heard footsteps on the staircase. I never saw anything, and had just decided that it was your wife, since you had told us you were getting ready for Christmas, and I figured she may have gone to get something from the attic. That room made me very dizzy, by the way. I don't know if you noticed me holding my head for a minute. That's never happened to me before - and after we left that room I was fine. I don't know if it is just the way the house isn't exactly level or what. Anyway, I never saw anything... I just assumed I was scared! The ghost walk had convinced me that I never wanted to set foot on your lawn, much less in your house. As soon as we got back in the car, my husband looked at me and said, 'Did you see the man in the black suit looking down on us from the attic when we were in the Front Parlor?' Now, I was paler than I usually am. I told him no, but I thought I had felt like someone was looking at us from up there. He then went on to tell me that the figure walked down the staircase while we were in the Game Room, and down that little hall. He didn't want to mention it at the time since this isn't a spirit that has ever been reported as being seen around. But he is absolutely sure of what he saw. He wondered if it could have been an early owner of the home."

Although the attic has never been occupied like the rest of the house, and the stairs are new to the 1990s, they both seem to be the focus of some of the supernatural activity in the house... a fact that continues to interest us.

Losing Time

While I don't have concrete explanations for most of the things that happen at The Grove, for many of them, I have at least an educated guess. For example, I assume that not only is the Lady in White a former owner of the house, but because of the path she takes, I believe it must be Minerva Stilley, the original lady of the house... something that I talked about in a previous chapter.

There have been a few things, however, that have happened that I have absolutely no explanation for. One of them I can't even guess at: it was losing time, a very strange phenomenon that has happened to me occasionally at The Grove.

Here's the way that it happened the first time. Tami had turned in for the evening, and I was staying up for another half-hour or so to do a little writing. It's not unusual for me to do that – sometimes I get my best writing done when the house is dark and quiet. I glanced up at the clock, and it said ten-thirty-something. I remember thinking, "Okay, half an hour and I'll stop what I'm doing and go to bed."

I'd written maybe a paragraph, looked up again, and the clock showed after midnight. Somehow a couple of hours had disappeared. I was perplexed, because the one thing that I was most sure of is that I hadn't fallen asleep. But I hadn't simply

169

lost track of time, either – I had written only a few sentences in very short order, yet somehow two hours had instantly gone by.

Confused by the whole thing, I just went to bed. The next day, it was still very fresh on my mind so I did some research and found that this kind of thing has happened to many people.

I read where folks have lost time while doing the most ordinary of things – even driving down the road. One account that I found involved a man driving his car down the highway about fifteen minutes from his exit. He was listening to a song, and in looking around, suddenly saw that he was about fifteen minutes *past* his exit. Looking down at the clock in the dash of the car, over an hour had passed. He had no memory of the time passing; if he had simply fallen prey to road hypnosis, he should have been much further down the highway, but the strangest thing was that the same song was still playing without interruption.

I kid you not – if you do a little research on the losing time phenomenon, you will find that it simply doesn't make any sense on any level... except maybe to physicists.

Explanations range from quantum physics events like time slips or dimensional slips, all the way to alien abduction. While I didn't believe that I'd been the guest of some alien spacecraft, I still couldn't explain what happened to me.

Clinical psychologists have documented cases of missing time – from hours to days or weeks – and they blame something called Dissociative Identity Disorder, or possibly Dissociative Amnesia. Either way, both are hard-core mental illnesses, and I don't seem to have displayed any of the traits of either, so I'm probably okay there... although, if you ask my wife and friends if I'm crazy, they might have to think about it before answering.

When a losing time episode happened again, I was, of course, more aware of all the possibilities from the research that I'd done. It was the same thing all over again – Tami had gone to bed, I was staying up to get a little more work done, and in the blink of an eye a couple of hours were suddenly gone.

I really would love to say that I'd woken up slumped down over my keyboard, drool oozing from the corner of my mouth, and that I had obviously fallen asleep… but that simply wasn't the case.

It even happened while I was writing this book. Tami had a day that was full of meetings and paperwork, and was exhausted. She went to bed at 10:15 that evening, and I thought that I could easily get in an hour's work before I turned in. I sat down at the computer, wrote about a page, and thought, "Wow, that didn't take long – I'm going to get a lot done!" But then I looked at the clock to see that it was ten minutes until midnight.

I'm aware that skeptics will say that I'd simply lost track of time, or fallen asleep, or gotten so wrapped up in my work that I didn't notice how much time had passed. While I truly understand why people would want to assume that, it simply isn't the case. With each time that it's happened, I've become more aware of the fact that time simply disappeared.

Although (thankfully) it's not a common occurrence, this has happened a number of times, with no explanation that I can imagine or find.

It's easy to show you what happened to me. Simply look at the clock right now, read the next section of this chapter, and then look at the clock again… but instead of the few minutes that it took to read it, imagine that two hours have passed. It was that quick and seamless for me.

The Mischievous Spirit of the Grove

One of our spirits is not only very interactive, he's very mischievous as well. Although we have no idea who he is, he seems to hang out in the Kitchen and the Den.

171

We assume that it's a male spirit because he seems to love to pick on the ladies, although he has picked on men as well... including me.

When we first bought the house, we'd stacked a lot of boxes in the Kitchen. We wanted to go through them slowly as we put things in their new places, but we also needed room to navigate that room for cooking, using the sink to run water for cleaning, and so forth.

I therefore set out to move as many of these boxes as possible out into the Side Gallery – the hallway that was once a porch. It was a tedious task, but I got into a rhythm: pick up a box, open the door from the Kitchen into the Side Gallery, walk out, and set it down. I'd then open the door back up and walk into the Kitchen, and start the process all over again. The door had an automatic closer so it would shut behind me each time.

I'd been working for about fifteen minutes, when I set a box down and turned the knob to open the door – but it wouldn't budge. I walked the length of the Side Gallery, came through the Stairwell, the Game Room, the Den, and finally got back into the Kitchen to find that the deadbolt had been thrown.

Unlocking it, I started the process again, and after another fifteen minutes or so, the same thing happened again... someone had thrown the deadbolt from inside the Kitchen. I was the only one in the house at that time, so as I made the long trek back around that second time, I was fussing at the house something fierce. I think that only encouraged the mischievous spirit, though, because it happened several times before I finished moving the boxes.

Over all the years that we've owned The Grove, that has continued to occasionally happen – usually when it's the most inconvenient! He loves locking us out of the Kitchen.

He's messed with our friends on occasion as well. Our friend Angie comes to visit periodically, and when she's come to visit in the past without her family along, we've simply made a bed for her on the couch in the Den.

One evening she came up for the weekend, and we hadn't seen her for a while, so we were staying up late talking, just getting caught up in general on life, jobs, family, etc.

It was getting into the wee morning hours when Angie stretched out on the couch and pulled the covers up. "You guys stay up as late as you'd like," she said, "but I'm exhausted and need to get some sleep."

We told her that we needed to turn in as well, so Tami headed for the Bedroom, and I stopped long enough to turn off the lights in the room so that they wouldn't bother Angie.

As I was leaving, I heard her cautiously say, "Wait a minute…"

I stuck my head back in and asked if she was okay, and she said, "Something just sat down on my legs. I can't move my legs!"

That concerned me, so I turned a lamp on, and asked, "Angie, are you having some kind of medical crisis like a stroke or something?"

She shook her head. "No, no, nothing like that. I can feel my legs, I just can't move them because something is sitting on them."

I looked over onto the covers, expecting to see a butt-print or something like that, but nothing was there. I asked, "Well, are you scared?"

She paused for a moment, thinking about it, and then said, "No, I'm not." After another moment she added, "I've always figured that with all the ghost stories from The Grove, it would only be a matter of time before something happened to me. I'm such a big chicken, that I figured I'd go screaming into the night when it did… but you know, now that it's happening it's not scary, it's just interesting."

"That's what we can't make people understand!" I said. "It's not scary – it really is just interesting!" I was delighted to hear that she wasn't freaked out by the supernatural occurrence. "Okay," I continued, "I'll go get Tami and we'll stand behind you and each grab a shoulder. We'll pull you out from under whatever it is."

"Are you kidding?" she said. "I want to see what happens next! You guys go on to bed."

I walked into the Bedroom, and Tami had already turned in. "What's wrong with Angie?" she asked.

"Something's sitting on her feet," I said, very matter-of-factly.

She digested that for a minute, and asked, "Is she okay with that?"

"She seems to be," I said, and crawled under the covers.

The next morning when we got up, Angie was already cooking breakfast in the Kitchen. "What happened?" I asked.

"About ten minutes after you left, there was a very pronounced movement off my legs, and the weight was gone." Whatever it was, she had a great attitude about it.

Probably the most embarrassing thing that's happened in the Den was back when The Grove was on the Candlelight Tour of Homes. As I've mentioned before, it's a Christmas tour of homes where the Historic Jefferson Foundation chooses four homes to open their doors to the public. You buy one ticket from the Foundation and get to tour all the homes which are lit by candlelight, decorated for Christmas, and staffed by docents in period costume to explain the history of the house.

The Grove has been honored to be on the tour twice. The first time, we were putting up our decorations, setting out candles around the house, and I was writing scripts for our friends who were going to be docents. As I was working on them, Tami walked up, looked over my shoulder, and said, "We're going to be on this tour with three other houses, and none of them are going to be telling ghost stories. For once in our lives, can we be like everyone else?"

I laughed and said, "That sounds like a good idea." We left off the ghost stories, and for the first two weekends in December that year, we only told the history of the house.

We had about three thousand people come through – it was a great fundraiser for the Foundation, and we were happy to help out.

The tour is on Thursday, Friday and Saturday evenings so that the candlelight shows up. On Sunday morning, went to the Bakery restaurant in Jefferson for breakfast – the Kitchen was so decorated that we couldn't dare use it.

As we sat in one of the booths enjoying our bacon, eggs, and toast, a couple came up to us. The lady said, "Do you guys own The Grove?"

I told her that we did, and she smiled and said, "I thought that I recognized you. We toured your house last night on the Candlelight Tour of Homes; they pointed out the owners, and I thought that looked like you two."

"Well that was us," I said. "I hope that you enjoyed the tour."

"We did," the lady replied, and then a quizzical look crossed her face. "I have to ask you, though: is your house haunted?"

I thought, "Oh great, what now?" but I just smiled and said, "Well, The Grove has its share of ghost stories, I guess... why?"

She went on to explain that they had parked in front of the house for the Candlelight Tour. There was a line to get in, and since about fifteen people at a time were being let in, they stood in line with the other strangers that had come up about the same time.

When they finally got to go inside, she said that they went through the house on the tour, and when they were back in the Den, she was standing there listening to the docent over by the Christmas tree giving the history of that part of the house.

Suddenly, she felt someone pop her on her bottom! Looking around, she saw that her husband was across the room, so she said that she figured, "Oh my gosh, one of these strangers had touched my bottom!"

Looking around, however, she quickly realized that no one else was even near her.

I was horrified and apologized profusely. When we finished eating we went back home, and I went straight into the Den. I shook my finger at the ceiling, and said, "I just heard that a woman got popped on the rear last night! That cannot happen – you must respect the ladies!"

Thankfully, that hasn't happened again, so maybe the mischievous spirit paid attention to me.

Although I do remember having a group of the "Red Hat" ladies on the tour one day, and when I was telling them that story, one of them said, "Oh, can't we suspend your rule for one day?"

They all giggled at the thought, but I laughed and said, "No – don't encourage this guy, whoever he is!"

He has also made his presence known by tapping people on the shoulder, calling their name from out in the hallway, and stroking their hair.

An example of the latter happened one tour after we'd moved into the Den. We were all standing in a circle, and as I was talking, suddenly a lady squealed and jumped.

I said, "Are you okay?" It had startled all of us in the room.

After a moment, she said, "I'm sorry. I was standing here listening to you, and I felt my friend stroking my hair." There was a fellow standing next to her that looked as confused as I was.

"Anyway, I thought, 'Oh, here we are on a romantic trip to Jefferson, and he's flirting with me!' I looked over to smile at him, and he had his phone out taking a picture, using both hands – he couldn't have been messing with my hair!"

Everyone laughed and the lady smiled nervously, but I just shook my head and thought, "the mischievous guy strikes again!"

There's something about the tour that seems to fascinate him – perhaps it's having strangers in who have come for the sole purpose of seeing his house.

I remember one tour where we were in the Den, and I was telling some stories, when a young lady jumped just as her necklace hit the floor. All eyes were on her as she stooped to pick it up and examine it.

"Is everything all right?" I asked her.

She didn't reply for a moment, studying the chain and pendant, and finally said, "Someone undid the clasp on my necklace!"

Before I could say anything, she had turned around to see who was there, but no one had been standing near her.

I always try to find an explanation for things that happen, so I laughed and said, "Oh, well, you must not have closed it properly when you put it on."

She wasn't amused. "No way," she said, shaking her head. "I've had it on since I first got dressed this morning, and we've been walking all over town. It would have come off then, not when I was standing perfectly still."

After a minute she added, "Besides, I felt someone touch the back of my neck. Whoever it was, well, he undid the clasp."

There was some nervous laughter, and I said, "I guess the mischievous spirit of The Grove took a liking to you and wanted to flirt a little."

One of her friends helped her put it back on, and I continued with the tour. When I told Tami about it later on, she said, "Well, you could make a case that it just wasn't fastened, and finally came undone."

I couldn't help but smile. "Yeah, except for the fact that it's happened on other occasions, and will probably happen again!"

As I said before, we have no idea who he is. A lot of his exploits occur in the Den, which is a new room not added until 1870. He also hangs out in the Kitchen, though, which was built as a stand-alone building in 1861 when the house was first constructed. There's no real clue as to who he might be… but he certainly seems to be enjoying himself.

Electrical Interference

We've had so many instances of electrical problems at The Grove that they could fill an entire chapter. The interesting thing is that they always happen to visitors, never to us. Our batteries don't suddenly die, our electronic equipment doesn't fail, we enjoy a very normal existence with our household gear.

Our visitors, however, have had quite a different experience. Here are a few representative stories, although they have happened for years, and continue to occasionally happen to this day.

We received an email from someone who said, "While we were in front of your home on the Ghost Walk, the batteries in my camera drained, and I had just put in new ones just before we started. A teenage girl also had the same thing happen to her at the exact same time. She was looking at my camera screen to see if mine was working, but it wasn't. She had been standing beside me while we were both trying to take pictures of the house. Our batteries died at the same time."

That's strangely similar to what happened to the two paranormal investigators who were at The Grove with the Showtime crew that I talked about in a previous chapter.

A guest came on The Grove tour and had yet another battery incident, this time in the Den. Here's what happened, in her own words: "When I toured The Grove last Saturday I had to change the batteries... and you helped open the compartment on my camera that wouldn't open for me, for whatever reason. I had just put in new batteries just before the tour; they should have lasted longer than that." I remember that not only had her batteries died, but she couldn't even open the compartment to change them – something that she indicated was usually a very simple process. I started trying to help, and we did finally get it open. The problem with the compartment flap was interesting, but not as much as the fact that brand new batteries kept dying.

She also had some electrical issues in the Front Parlor of The Grove, as she reported, "Also, when we were just getting started in the room with the 'strange' corner, my mother was holding one of my recorders and turned to me since it had stopped. I thought she may have accidentally hit a button. I hit record again for her. Then I noticed that the recorder I was holding was on pause. So I also had to get the one I was using recording again. That was a little weird, too." Perhaps both she and her mother happened to hit buttons at the same time on their audio recorders to stop them, and that's perfectly understandable... but in looking at her experiences over the weekend with her electrical devices, it certainly appears that she was having a rash of electronics-related experiences like so many people do at The Grove.

Another day we had a family on the tour. As we were starting, I said the same thing that I always do: "If you brought your camera, please take all the photos that you'd like, but if there's anything interesting we'd love to see it." One of the ladies went back to the car, and came back a little puzzled - not only was her phone dead (which she used as a camera), but so was her iPad, both of which had been freshly charged. Electrical problems abound with visitors to The Grove!

Voices at The Grove

One of the first things that happened to us when we bought the house was an audible phenomenon – footsteps.

One night early on we were getting dressed to go out for dinner with friends. I was ready before my wife, so I stepped out onto the Side Gallery. Suddenly, I heard the distinct, loud pacing of footsteps across the Front Parlor. At that time, there was little furniture there, so I assumed that our friends had knocked on the door without us hearing, and just let themselves in. I stuck my head back into the Bedroom and said, "Hey, they're up front – I'm going to go tell them that we'll be ready in just a minute." I walked through the Side Gallery, still hearing the pacing up front, and then rounded the corner of the Stairwell expecting to see our friends. Instead, there was only an empty room. When I checked the front door, the deadbolt was thrown – there was no way that anyone could have come into the front room. Still, I had heard footsteps there as sure as I'd heard my own walking in the Side Gallery.

Those were the first of many, many times we have heard – and continue to hear – footsteps in the house.

That isn't as interesting as other audible occurrences, though. You see, we sometimes hear voices at The Grove.

Of course, I'm aware that when someone claims to be hearing voices, it usually means that they're crazy. These voices aren't in our heads, however… they're at The Grove.

My dad didn't believe in anything such as ghosts, but before my father became sick and eventually died, he told me something that I'll never forget.

When we first purchased The Grove, we renovated many rooms of the house, including the Kitchen. In fact, we took that particular room down to the lapboard on the studs and started from scratch.

We had a table saw, all of our tools, and some scrap lumber out on the front porch; it was more or less our workshop.

I was working on a project and needed a 2x4 cut to two feet. My dad said, "I'm not busy – I'll go do it." He disappeared through the Kitchen door and came back about fifteen minutes later with the wood cut to the exact, correct size.

It wasn't until years later that he confessed, "You know, something happened to me at The Grove that I've spent a lot of time trying to figure out, but just can't. I guess that it's about time that I told you about it. We were working on the Kitchen, and I was going to cut a 2x4 out on the porch. I walked from the Kitchen up to the front of the house, and as I was going into the Dining Room, I heard a conversation taking place in the Front Parlor. I wondered how you guys had gotten ahead of me to get up there, but when I looked over, the room was empty. No one was there, but I swear to you there were two people talking when I walked in. It was so real that I knew it had to be a couple of you, so I even backtracked to the Kitchen to see if you were still there – which you were. I can't explain it, but I definitely heard a conversation in the Front Parlor even though no one was there."

I think this bothered Dad, because while he was so vehemently against the idea of ghosts, he'd definitely experienced something supernatural at The Grove.

Probably the voice that I hear most often is a woman calling my name, and usually when I'm shaving. I've been in our bathroom, looking in the mirror with shaving cream all over my face. As I wet my razor and start the routine, I've heard a woman's voice call, "Mitchel!" I always assume that it's my wife, so I'll turn around, shaving cream all over my face, and call back, "What?" When she doesn't answer, I'll walk through the house looking for her and calling her name, razor in one hand and the other under my chin to catch any dripping shaving cream, and when I finally find her I'll say, "What is it?"

"What are you talking about?" she'll always answer.

"You called me!" I'll say, and after seeing how confused she was, I'll shake my head and walk away, saying, "Nevermind..." It seems whoever is doing that takes immense pleasure in watching me trek through The Grove with shaving cream all over my face.

Even our guests on the tour have experienced an audible interaction with our spirits. More than once, I've led a group into the Den, and as I was telling some of the stories from that part of the house, one fellow kept looking back over his shoulder into the hallway.

I finally stopped and asked him if anything strange was going on, and he said, "Twice now I've heard someone call my name from out in the hall, but nobody's out there!"

That same thing has been repeated any number of times on the tour, and people always smile and give a nervous laugh, but keep looking over their shoulder as the tour continues.

Electronic Voice Phenomenon

Electronic Voice Phenomenon, or EVP as it is commonly known, is the capturing of mysterious voices or sounds on an audio recording that were not audible when the recording was made. Some people attribute these things to the idea that spirits find it easier to create noise that is inaudible to the human ear, but which can be picked up by recording devices, which can detect a much wider audible range. Paranormal researchers look for EVP when investigating a location that is reported to have supernatural activity... and this kind of thing has been captured any number of times at The Grove over the years.

Several have come from paranormal investigation groups who have visited the house, and others have come from visitors on the tour. I always look forward to getting emails with EVPs attached.

Probably my favorite happened during a tour one day, and I was leading the group from the parlor into the Dining Room. One of our guests happened to have a voice recorder, and when they went back and listened to the recording, found something very interesting.

I was speaking, and said, "Frank and Minerva lived here for about twenty years, raised two sons here, and then something terrible happened..." As I talk, the floors are creaking as everyone moves to the Dining Room, and you can hear a whispered voice that says "Leave me alone..."

Since I received the EVP not long after the tour, I remembered that day, and I certainly didn't hear a voice like that. It is probably the best example of Electronic Voice Phenomenon that I've ever heard.

Odors in the Air

There are several distinct odors that show at The Grove – one is the smell of pungent body odor, another is pipe tobacco, and a third is perfume.

The most memorable occurrence of the body odor, at least to me, was one evening when The Grove was on the Candlight Tour of Homes in Jefferson. Our friends and family were serving as docents for the tour, and everyone was in period costume. Our friend who was in the Dining Room said that a group of people came through on the tour, and after they left, the distinct smell of body odor was hanging in the air. She thought, "Wow, someone in that last group needs a bath!"

As the next few groups came through the room, the odor did not dissipate. Our friend was becoming paranoid and thinking, "Oh, my, could it be me?" During a break in the activity, she walked over to the parlor where our friend Angie was docenting and said, "I'm embarrassed to ask, but I have to. Do I stink?"

Angie leaned over, took a healthy sniff, and said, "No, I'm getting a whiff of perfume, but that's it. You're fine!"

I was on the front porch, so our friend came out and told me what was going on. I walked into the Dining Room since we didn't have any guests at the moment, and said, "Will whoever is hanging out in here please leave? To be honest, you smell, and we don't need you here tonight!"

The scent of body odor faded, and was gone for the rest of the evening. It does occasionally come back – sometimes in the Dining Room, but also in the Game Room or the Den. But always in the rooms on the east side of the house, though.

The pipe tobacco shows up in the east side of the house as well. Usually in the Dining Room, but it has been found in the Game Room as well. It is a sweet scent, and unmistakable when it happens.

One day on a tour, I led the group into the Dining Room and suddenly picked up on the tobacco – it actually smells quite good. One of my rules for the tour is that if I detect something supernatural is going on, I don't call attention to it. I don't want the tour to seem contrived or staged, so I just go on like nothing is happening. One of the guests, however, sniffed the air and said, "Who smokes Prince Albert?"

I simply answered, "What do you mean?"

"That smell is Prince Albert pipe tobacco," she said. "My dad smoked it his entire life, and I could pick it out anywhere!"

I said, "Well, we don't smoke, or allow smoking in the house, so it's nothing from this world."

Everyone laughed, but personally, I was delighted. I didn't know who this spirit was, but at least now I knew what he smoked – Prince Albert!

The other common odor is that of perfume. It shows up here and there, sometimes just a slight whiff, and on other occasions is very strong. We're not sure what kind it is, but Tami seems to be allergic to it. On many occasions we've been sitting in the Den watching television or quietly working, when the perfumed spirit comes in and Tami starts sneezing uncontrollably. Over the years we've learned to simply ask, "Will whoever is in here please leave? Your perfume is causing a problem."

Interestingly enough, the spirit leaves without pomp, circumstance, or fanfare, and everything is back to normal in short order. Again, we have no idea who this might be.

Nocturnal Visitations

I think that because of all the horror movies that have come out over the years, people assume that most things happen at night. That's simply not the case, however; we've had experiences in the morning, in the afternoon, and in the evening as well.

That said, we have had a number of nocturnal experiences over the years. One of the most interesting stories, at least for me, happened in the middle of the night.

We have basset hounds, and their dog beds are down on the floor, although they've been known to climb up in bed with us. In case they have to go to the bathroom in the middle of the night, we keep one of the doors to our bedroom open. The French doors are old, and squeak when you move them.

One night the squeaking of one of the doors woke me, and I actually sat up in bed. In the ambient light coming in from around the window curtains, I could see that the door was slowly opening up. My first thought was, "Why was that door closed?"

That was quickly followed by, "And who is opening it?" It opened all the way, and came to rest by the dresser. Looking around, I saw that Tami was asleep next to me, the dogs were in their beds, and there was no other sound in the house. I knew that if we had an intruder the dogs would be going crazy, so after sitting there a minute, I laid back down. As I drifted off to sleep, I said, "Whoever opened the door, please don't mess with me. I want to get some sleep."

The rest of the evening was quiet.

Tami had a more dramatic experience one evening, however. She awoke about four o'clock one morning because she thought that she heard something. She rose up in bed, and could see that there were a number of people walking up and down the hallway in front of our bedroom. They were dressed in old fashioned clothing and seemed to have a glow about them, so she recognized immediately that something beyond the natural world was happening.

After all these years of living at The Grove and with all the experiences that we've had, she wasn't scared. She was instead just curious.

As she watched, a few of the people came into the Bedroom and continued into the bathroom, although one lady paused and looked at us there in bed. She moved on, and as ridiculous as this might seem, Tami just laid back down, turned, over, and went to sleep.

I can imagine people saying, "Oh, that would terrify me!" or "I'd have to jump up and turn on the light!" We've lived at The Grove a long time, though, and had many supernatural experiences, so it was actually kind of normal in our world.

For me, well, I can't imagine being an ambulance paramedic – you see people who have been killed in car crashes, been the victim of terrible attacks, and lost their lives in horrible ways. I could never get used to that. But for many people in that profession, all those things are simply routine and part of their daily lives.

That's the way that the supernatural is for us. We're around it so much that it doesn't frighten or disturb us – we just feel blessed that we get a peek into the other side on a fairly regular basis!

Odds & Ends

This has been a catch-all chapter for things that really didn't fit anywhere else, and I could probably go on and on. After all these years of living at The Grove, the thing that probably fascinates me the most is why the spirits come across in such different ways. Why does the lady in the Front Parlor corner come across as just a feeling, when the Lady in White and the Garden Guy look as real as you or I?

We go through periods of seeing a lot of shadow people activity, and other times when we hear footsteps and voices in different parts of the house.

I know that the day will eventually come when I understand everything about the other side, but for now, I'm not rushing that. I simply enjoy experiencing all the supernatural events at The Grove.

The Future of The Grove

    This is a melancholy way to wrap up the story of The Grove, but I think that it's right and proper.

    As the current owners of The Grove, it's hard to imagine that anyone besides us will own the house. But truth be told, a day will come when my wife and I will pass on and become part of that other side, and someone else will take over the ownership of The Grove. Hopefully, they will preserve the house as it is, and won't modernize or alter it. As it is, The Grove has a certain amount of legal protection, since it has been listed on the National Register of Historic Places by the United States Department of the Interior. By the way, on the historic registers, they name homes for the family who built it, and the family who lived there the longest. The Grove is therefore listed as the "Stilley-Young House."

STILLEY-YOUNG HOUSE

405 MOSELEY STREET
BUILT IN 1861

LISTED IN THE
NATIONAL REGISTER OF HISTORIC PLACES
BY THE UNITED STATES
DEPARTMENT OF THE INTERIOR

It has also been designated as a Registered Texas Historical Landmark by the Texas Historical Commission.

In addition, the State of Texas has also designated the Grove (a.k.a. Stilley-Young House) as a State Antiquities Landmark, joining other historic places such as the Alamo, the Texas State Capitol building, the Galveston Sea Wall, and the San Jacinto Battlefield to name but a few.

With both a state and a federal historical marker, and the State Antiquities Landmark designation, The Grove is protected under the National Historic Preservation Act (NHPA; Public Law 89-665; 54 U.S.C. 300101 et seq.), which is legislation intended to preserve historical and archaeological sites in the United States of America.

Hopefully it will stand for many years, decades, and even centuries to come.

A Final Word on the Haunting

We've talked to countless people who have had supernatural experiences at The Grove, and they come from all walks of life: old and young, and of all races, nationalities and religions. People have had encounters with the spirit world at the house that include police officers, military personnel, educators, doctors, businessmen, scientists, and pretty much anyone that you can imagine.

After all the ghost stories that I've told, and with all the things that have been documented about The Grove over the years – and through many different owners and visitors – one thing that I believe is that unlike some Hollywood horror movie, no spirit is stuck at the house and "can't make it to the other side."

Instead, as I have previously mentioned, I believe that former residents are simply coming back for an occasional visit – some more often than others – just to check out the house that they loved so much.

After living at The Grove for all these years, that makes sense to me. After all, we've helped preserve the house, have gotten a lot of historical recognition for the place, and we tell its history along with its ghost stories every weekend. In doing that, though, we feel that we honor the previous owners and their lives at the house.

But still, I know that a time will eventually come when Tami and I pass on, and The Grove will be taken over by new owners. This bothers me; I wonder whether they will keep the dining table that belonged to the Youngs, or replace the closet in the Game Room that came from Minerva Stilley's armoire. Will they keep Louise Young's sink in the Kitchen that, although scarred up, has been there since the 1930s? These kinds of things give me pause.

One afternoon when Patrick Hopkins, the seventh owner of the house and the chef who had a restaurant there, was visiting we were sitting on the front porch talking about such matters, and he just smiled and said, "You know how much I love this house – well, I was worried about the same kinds of things. It took years to sell it, but when it did, the house had picked you guys who love it like I do.

He reached out, patted my on the shoulder, and said, "Don't worry. The Grove will take care of itself after you're gone." And hopefully it will. Maybe I'll even be there to see it.

You see, Patrick tells me that he used to sit on the bench beside the front door, enjoying a cigarette and waiting for guests to come in.

He says that once he's gone, we'll walk into the front of the house and smell cigarette smoke, and that will be him.

Me, I'll be out on the front porch. I love sitting out there in the rocking chair, especially in the morning with a cup of coffee. Whoever owns The Grove a hundred years from now will talk about the "rocking chair ghost," where the chair slowly begins to move back and forth and there's the smell of fresh coffee in the air. That's going to be me.

www.ingramcontent.com/pod-product-compliance
Lightning Source LLC
Chambersburg PA
CBHW070350090426
42733CB00009B/1365